ALIVE
GOSPEL SEXUALITY
FOR STUDENTS

ALIVE

GOSPEL SEXUALITY FOR STUDENTS

Study Guide with Leader's Notes

Harvest USA

New
Growth
Press

WWW.NEWGROWTHPRESS.COM

New Growth Press, Greensboro, NC 27404
www.newgrowthpress.com
Copyright © 2018 Harvest USA

Scripture quotations are taken from *The Holy Bible, English Standard Version.*® Copyright © 2000; 2001 by Crossway Bibles, a division of Good News Publishers. Used by permission. All rights reserved.

Cover Design: Faceout Books, faceoutstudio.com
Interior Typesetting and eBook: Lisa Parnell, lparnell.com

ISBN: 978-1-945270-91-8 (Print)
ISBN: 978-1-945270-92-5 (eBook)

Printed in the United States of America

25 24 23 22 21 20 19 18   1 2 3 4 5

CONTENTS

Student's Guide

Leader's Guide

STUDENT'S GUIDE

INTRODUCTION

Alive: Gospel Sexuality for Students is a ten-week, small group study that covers many of the major issues concerning human sexuality. All of us are clamoring for a steadfastness and a hope in the world in which we live, but despite the sexual chaos of the world around us—and the chaos we experience in our own sexuality—Jesus is Lord and Savior.

Here is the vision behind *Alive: Gospel Sexuality for Students.*

THE VISION

We can often feel as if the gospel has little relevance in day-to-day living, but we believe that the risen and ascended Lord makes all the difference in every area of our lives. This study seeks to unpack and apply the rich truths of believers' union with Christ to the particulars of human sexuality. In other words, believers have died with Christ and now live with him, and by his Spirit, Christ provides both the motivation and power for believers to use their sexuality for his glory. Nothing, not even our sexuality, is outside his transforming work and power. Here is the vision from the apostle Paul:

> If then you have been raised with Christ, seek the things that are above, where Christ is, seated at the right hand of God. Set your minds on things that are above, not on things that are on earth. For you have died, and your life is hidden with Christ in God. When Christ who is your life appears, then you also will appear with him in glory. (Colossians 3:1–4)

We want to talk about the issues that are part of our everyday world. But we also want to lead you toward robust, deep, and strengthening theological content that will help you follow Jesus in the area of sexuality. As you hopefully identify with the content, our prayer is that the content will in turn challenge you to grow further in your Christian walk.

1

THE STUDY

We have designed this study to be used in a small group that is conversational and interactive but also guided by a leader. There is no homework for you to do outside of each week's lesson, although it might be helpful for you to go over the next lesson a week in advance to write down your thoughts.

Each week focuses mainly on discussion and application. This means that you will get the most out of the study as you engage in the discussions. There will, however, be times of awkward silence and intense floor staring. Hopefully, through the intentional time set aside to address these issues each week, conversation and discussion will flow more naturally as the study progresses.

So, what can you expect each week?

EACH WEEK

Most weeks contain the elements listed below, though some do not. Here is a general outline of each lesson:

1. The Scenario

We begin each week with a scenario that sets up the main topic for that day. This scenario is meant to be a simple, quick way to break some of the tension and to introduce the issue at hand in a way that does not put everyone on the spot, hopefully creating a safer atmosphere to discuss it.

2. Scenario Reflective Questions

Each week we give some reflective questions on the scenario. The purpose is threefold: to help you think critically about the issues, to help you connect the scenario to topics discussed in previous weeks, and to help you enter into the scenario yourselves, connecting your own experience with that of the person(s) in the scenario.

3. The Issue

This is an opportunity for you to connect specific sexual issues with biblical, Christ-centered truth. The group will read and discuss several Scripture passages.

4. The Issue in Life

This section is very practical, helping you to think through how the Scriptures and Jesus interact with particular sexual issues in your own life. The goal is for you to think through ways you can walk with Jesus as you, or someone you might know, wrestles with particular sins and sufferings in everyday life.

5. The Point

This same question every week asks you to think through the week's main point. The group will have multiple answers, and that is okay.

KEY TRUTHS AND CONCEPTS

This study is based on certain key, biblical truths that guide our discussion of the gospel and sexuality. There is also a glossary in the back to further reinforce these truths. Spend some time familiarizing yourself with these concepts.

Key Biblical Truths

1. The Human Heart

In the Bible, it is the human heart that defines people as individuals and is the mover of faith and trust. What goes on in people's hearts is what the Lord is most concerned with in their lives. It can even be thought of as their nature. What people's hearts desire and love leads to their thoughts and actions. Deuteronomy 6:5 says, "You shall love the LORD your God with all your heart and with all your soul and with all your might." Romans 10:10 says, "For with the heart one believes and is justified, and with the mouth one confesses and is saved."

Human hearts, naturally, have rejected God and have trusted in other things besides him for life and salvation. Beginning with Adam and Eve, people have rebelled against God. Their natural hearts are not neutral or basically good but are evil and corrupt (Genesis 8:21; Jeremiah 17:9). Not only are human hearts naturally evil, the Bible even calls people "dead in" their "trespasses and sins" (Ephesians 2:1).

When people put their faith in Jesus, however, he makes them alive—new creations.

Their hearts are radically transformed. The new nature of a believer is holy and clean (Ezekiel 36:26), although he or she will still struggle with sin on this side of eternity.

2. The New Creation

When people come to Jesus by faith, they become new creations (2 Corinthians 5:17). They are given the Spirit of God (Romans 8:9–11), who makes them alive in Christ (Ephesians 2:1–10). Believers are part of the new creation now, as they await the re-creation of all things in the future (Revelation 21—22).

3. Union with Christ

This might be the most important concept of this study. The reason why believers are new creations in Christ is because Jesus Christ was raised from the dead, the "first fruits" of new creation (Romans 6:4; 1 Corinthians 15:20). He has passed through death into a new, transformed, imperishable life. Christians are united to Christ by the Spirit; their identity with the old creation and with Adam is broken as they share in Christ's death, and they are raised to new life with him (Colossians 3:1–4). Christians have a resurrected life in Christ now (Romans 6:1–4), and they will be resurrected in glory when he comes again (1 Corinthians 15). Christians are seated with Christ now (Ephesians 2:6), and they will reign with him for eternity. This can be put into a simple saying: So goes Christ, so go all who put their faith in him. As Paul said, "I have been crucified with Christ. It is no longer I who live, but Christ who lives in me. And the life I now live in the flesh I live by faith in the Son of God, who loved me and gave himself for me" (Galatians 2:20).

Because of what Christ has done for his people, and who they are in him, believers have undergone a fundamental identity shift from sinner to saint. Christians are brought back into relationship with God through Jesus (John 14:6). They are adopted as sons and daughters through the blood of Christ. He paid for their sins, and now they are fully forgiven (1 John 1:9; 4:10–11). They are set apart for him now and have peace with God for eternity (Romans 5:1), giving them total access to God as their Father (Romans 8:15–17).

4. Flesh and Spirit

Within believers, there remains something of the "flesh" (their old desires, their old sin patterns). Paul explains, "the desires of the flesh are against the Spirit, and the desires of the Spirit are against the flesh, for these are opposed to each other, to keep you from doing the things you want to do" (Galatians 5:17). But the flesh does not define a believer like it does an unbeliever. The Holy Spirit in the believer will have the upper hand and will complete the work that God started (Philippians 1:6).

Key Concepts

1. The Tree Metaphor

The Scriptures give us many places to go to understand people. In Luke 6:43–45, Jesus gives a helpful metaphor about people, where the most fundamental part of who they are is the heart, or seed of the tree.

We can expand Jesus's metaphor to take into account other aspects of human existence as well. The tree's seed is planted in soil that it cannot control. In the same way, people live in contexts that they cannot always control—and these correspond to the sufferings, hardships, and general things people can't control in life.

From people's hearts flow their desires (James 1:14–15). These can easily correspond to the roots of the tree. People seek to be nourished and fed through what they desire, just as roots seek out nutrients.

People's hearts, the context in which they live, and their desires ultimately form their worldview, corresponding to the tree's trunk. The trunk of the tree holds the tree up. In the same way, people's worldviews about God, themselves, and others hold them up and transform the way they live (Romans 1:22–25). People's behavior (the fruit) flows directly from their worldviews. What people really think about God, themselves, and other people always produces their actions and behaviors.

2. The Triad of Life

The Triad of Life is the way we live the Christian life. The Triad of Life consists of three things: faith, repentance, and love. When Jesus comes on to the scene, he says, "The time is fulfilled, and the kingdom of God is at hand; repent and believe in the gospel" (Mark 1:15). Repentance from sin and faith in Jesus are flip sides of the same coin. Both are required for people to be saved and transformed in Christ, and both are required every day in the lives of believers. Following from the first and second great commandments (Matthew 22:37–40), love for God and others forms the outward expression of the Christian life. Turning from sin and to Jesus in faith, as well as loving and serving God and others, characterize a believer's life.

One more thing before you jump in: The issues discussed in this study are extremely sensitive. You, or other students you know, will have baggage, fear, and shame when talking about them—as many, if not most, of the group has already experienced firsthand what will be discussed. We pray that the good news of Christ—that he has come to make new what was broken, to give life where there was death, to offer forgiveness and grace where there is sin, and to transform sinners into people who treasure him above all—becomes our sole hope as we journey forward.

We hope that as you discuss these matters, Christ will become more and more beautiful to everyone, and that your desire to follow him with your sexuality will increase week after week.

> Now may the God of peace who brought again from the dead our Lord Jesus, the great shepherd of the sheep, by the blood of the eternal covenant, equip you with everything good that you may do his will, working in us that which is pleasing in his sight, through Jesus Christ, to whom be glory forever and ever. Amen.
>
> Hebrews 13:20–21

WEEK ONE:
WHAT DOES GOD HAVE TO DO
WITH SEXUALITY?

These first three weeks will be different than the weeks to come, as they lay a broad foundation for understanding our sexuality and the complexity we experience as human beings. First, to understand our sexuality and what went wrong, we have to understand where it all began.

THE SCENARIO

> Then the man said, "This at last is bone of my bones and flesh of my flesh; she shall be called Woman, because she was taken out of Man." Therefore a man shall leave his father and his mother and hold fast to his wife, and they shall become one flesh. And the man and his wife were both naked and were not ashamed (Genesis 2:23–25).

SCENARIO REFLECTIVE QUESTIONS

1. Genesis 2:24 is the first mention of marriage in the Bible. Christians refer to this as the "covenant" of marriage. What might be the difference between a covenant and two people who make a commitment to live together? Which is safer, covenant or commitment? Why?

2. In the covenant relationship, "the man and his wife were both naked and were not ashamed." What does this tell you about life in the garden?

THE ISSUE: GENESIS 1:26–31; 2:15–17

1. Before God creates the covenant of marriage, what does God create in Genesis 1:26–27? What difference does it make to sexuality that God himself created, and created things "very good" in verse 31?

2. In Genesis 1:28, were sex or our sexuality created for a purpose or as an end in themselves? Explain.

3. What does Genesis 1:29–30 tell you about the character of God? What does God's character have to do with sex and sexuality?

4. What is a worldview? How might Adam and Eve have viewed each other, God, and the world around them given Genesis 1:26–31?

5. What does Genesis 2:15–17 tell us about the original relationship between Adam and God?

THE ISSUE IN LIFE

1. According to our culture, how do Christians view sex and sexuality? Looking back at question 3 in "The Issue," how does God's Word present sex and sexuality? Compare and contrast God's voice and our culture's voice on sex and sexuality.

2. Do you normally think about sex and sexuality with God in the mix? Explain.

3. What can we expect from life since God created human beings with sexual desire? Explain.

4. Practically, how can Christians live godly lives in light of their God-given sexual desires and sexuality?

THE POINT

Summarize, in your own words, one point from this week's lesson.

WEEK TWO:
WHAT WENT WRONG?

THE SCENARIO

Sam and Heather have been dating for a few months. Sam is pressuring Heather to go further physically in their relationship, saying things like, "Look. It's no big deal. Don't you want to take our relationship to the next level?"

Sarah has been feeling differently for years now. She has tried to get into the things that interest other girls, but she just cannot. She feels more at home with her dad and fixing cars, but she also listens, time and again, to her friends talk about their boyfriends and has started to pick up on something else. She feels attracted to other girls.

Mike rushes home every day. He is a loner with not many friends, much less a girlfriend. He anticipates his afternoons and thinks about them throughout his day, and finally, when school gets out, he longs to get home and into his room. As he sits alone, day after day, he views countless pornographic videos and images.

SCENARIO REFLECTIVE QUESTIONS

1. Let's think through the scenarios above. For Sam and Heather, why do you think Sam wants to go further physically? What are some desires he might have? How might Heather feel? What might be some of her desires?

2. For Sarah, how might she feel about not fitting in with the other girls? What things play into her feelings of not fitting in? Explain.

3. In light of using porn, how might Mike feel about himself? How might he feel about the world around him? How might he feel about others, especially girls?

THE ISSUE: GENESIS 1:27–28; 3:1–24; JOHN 14:6; MARK 1:14–15; MATTHEW 22:36–40

Genesis 1:27–28

1. How does the world think gender and sexual identity are formed? Why is it significant that God creates and has a specific design for these things?

Genesis 3:1–6

1. What do you think it means that the serpent "was more crafty than any other beast of the field that the LORD God had made"? What were the serpent's tactics in tempting Eve?

2. Thinking specifically about the scenario situations, how does sexual temptation make us doubt God and his intentions for us? What things might sexual temptation tell us about God's motives and character? Have you ever felt these tactics in action? Explain.

Genesis 3:7–13

1. In light of Adam's and Eve's rebellion, shame comes into the picture. What is shame? What does shame have to do with Adam's and Eve's hiding? What does shame have to do with sexual sin?

2. As well as shame, the concept of fear is introduced here. What is fear? What does that have to do with Adam's and Eve's hiding? What does fear have to do with sexual sin?

Genesis 3:14–19

1. In response to Adam's and Eve's rebellion, God curses them. What are the curses that God gives to Adam and Eve? What does this mean for humanity now?

2. What hope does God offer Adam and Eve? Why does this do away with man's fear and shame in relationship to God?

Genesis 3:20–24

1. Despite the curses that God gives, God covers Adam and Eve. What does this act have to do with shame (read 2 Corinthians 5:21)? What does this act reveal about God's character?

2. Why does God prevent Adam and Eve from eating from the Tree of Life? What does this reveal about God's character and plan?

John 14:6

1. Moving from Genesis to Jesus, what do you think it means for Jesus to be "the way, and the truth, and the life"?

2. Contrast Jesus's words in John 14:6 with the serpent's words in Genesis 3:1–5. What does this have to do with our sexuality?

Mark 1:14–15; Matthew 22:36–40

1. Mark 1:14–15 and Matthew 22:36–40 form what we call the Triad of Life: The Christian life is to be lived in faith (trusting in Christ as Savior), repentance (turning from sin and turning to God in faith), and love (loving God and others). Given man's rebellion against God and God's pursuit of man in Christ, how does sexual sin distort and ruin faith and repentance?

2. How does sexual sin destroy true love?

THE POINT

Summarize, in your own words, one point from this week's lesson.

WEEK THREE:
THE TREE METAPHOR

THE SCENARIO

This is the same scenario as last week. But this week, we will apply the Tree Metaphor to it.

In a youth group much like yours . . . Sam and Heather have been dating for a few months. Sam is pressuring Heather to go further physically in their relationship, saying things like, "Look. It's no big deal. Don't you want to take our relationship to the next level?"

Sarah has been feeling differently for years now. She has tried to get into the things that interest other girls, but she just cannot. She feels more at home with her dad and fixing cars, but she also listens, time and again, to her friends talk about their boyfriends and has started to pick up on something else. She feels attracted to other girls.

Mike rushes home every day. He is a loner with not many friends, much less a girlfriend. He anticipates his afternoons and thinks about them throughout his day, and finally, when school gets out, he longs to get home and into his room. As he sits alone, day after day, he views countless pornographic videos and images.

SCENARIO REFLECTIVE QUESTIONS

An understanding of the human person comes from a variety of places in the Scriptures. In Luke 6:43–45, Jesus gives a helpful metaphor about people, where the most fundamental part of who they are is the heart, or seed of the tree.

The tree's seed is planted in soil that it cannot control. In the same way, people live in contexts that they cannot always control, including the sufferings and hardships they experience in life.

From people's hearts flow their desires (James 1:14–15). These are the roots of the tree. People's desires are seeking nourishment from things around them. Just as roots seek soil full of nutrients, people desire and reach out for whatever they think might satisfy and/or save them.

19

People's hearts, the context in which they live, and their desires help to form their worldview, which corresponds to the tree's trunk. The trunk of the tree holds the tree up; in the same way, people's worldviews about God, themselves, and others hold them up and transform the way they live (Romans 1:22–25). People's behavior (the fruit) flows from their worldview. What people really think about God, themselves, and other people produces their actions and behaviors.

THE ISSUE: LUKE 6:43–45; ROMANS 10:10; PROVERBS 27:19; 2 CORINTHIANS 5:17; ECCLESIASTES 2:22–23; MATTHEW 16:24; JAMES 1:14–15; GALATIANS 5:16–17; ROMANS 1:22–25

Applying the Tree Metaphor

Luke 6:43–45; Romans 10:10

1. If you had to apply the Tree Metaphor to Sam and Heather's situation, what is the sinful fruit?

2. According to Romans 10:10 and beginning with the "seed" of the tree, why is Christ so concerned with our hearts? What do faith and trust have to do with sexual sin?

The Issue of Identity

Proverbs 27:19; 2 Corinthians 5:17

1. What are some things Proverbs 27:19 tells us about the heart, the seed of the human tree? How does the heart act as a reflective mirror? Explain.

2. What does 2 Corinthians 5:17 have to do with our hearts?

3. What do the terms "in Christ" and "new creation" in 1 Corinthians 5:17 have to do with sexual sin and identity? If a believer sins, does that mean he or she is not a Christian? Can the believer ever be ultimately defined by his or her sin? Explain.

Ecclesiastes 2:22–23; Matthew 16:24

1. Moving on to the soil of the tree, what do you think is the point of Ecclesiastes 2:22–23?

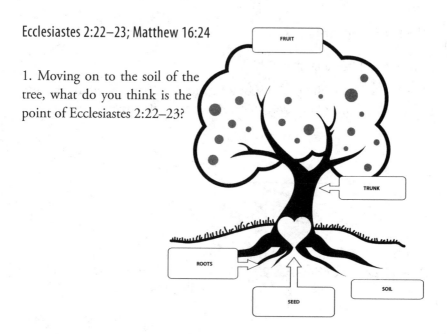

2. What are some specific things that have happened to you because you live in a fallen world? How is the soil of a tree like the sufferings we experience in life? What are some other sufferings Christians might face?

3. According to Matthew 16:24, what can the Christian expect from a life of following Christ? How does this match up to the category of the soil? Explain.

4. What are some sufferings that might be in play with Sarah?

James 1:14–15; Galatians 5:16–17

1. The roots of the tree are, by nature, searching for water and nourishment. The roots of a tree can correspond to our own desires. Connecting James 1:14–15 to what we have talked about so far, why are our natural desires not good or even neutral? What are some desires you can think of that would contribute to our sexuality? Explain.

2. According to Galatians 5:16–17, what spiritual dynamic is at work in the desires of a believer? What desires of both the flesh and the Spirit might be at work in both Sam and Heather?

Romans 1:22–25

1. What does the trunk of a tree do for the tree? How do our worldviews about God, ourselves, and other people act like the trunk of a tree? Explain.

2. Thinking about the trunk of the tree, what are some broken worldviews about God, ourselves, and others that Romans 1 brings up?

3. For Mike, what are some worldviews about God, himself, and others that might be in play?

4. In light of Christ, how do you think we should see God, ourselves, and others? Explain.

THE POINT

Summarize, in your own words, one point from this week's lesson.

WEEK FOUR:
PORNOGRAPHY

THE SCENARIO

This week, your leader will read the scenario aloud to you.

SCENARIO REFLECTIVE QUESTIONS

1. In thinking through the Tree Metaphor, what are some soil factors in this person's life? What are some good desires that this person might have? What are some worldviews that might be in play?

2. In what ways can you relate to this person's soil factors?

THE ISSUE: MATTHEW 5:27–30

1. How would you define pornography?

2. What do you think Jesus is most concerned about in these verses, and how does this relate to the Triad of Life? How do these verses encourage us to think about porn?

3. What other things, besides lust, do you think would cause someone to want to engage in pornography?

4. What are some harmful effects of pornography? How might porn affect the way we view ourselves, others, and God? How does porn harm other people?

THE ISSUE IN LIFE: ROMANS 6:6–14; HEBREWS 12:1–2; HEBREWS 10:24; HEBREWS 3:12–13

Romans 6:6–14

1. What do you think verses 6–7 mean? What hope does this offer to someone caught in the grasp of pornography?

2. Given verses 8–11, how does Paul encourage believers to view themselves? Explain.

3. In light of the believer's union with Christ, and from verses 12–13, how might someone who struggles with pornography not let sin "reign"? How might he or she not "present" his or her body "to sin as [an instrument] for unrighteousness" and "present" his or her body as an instrument "for righteousness"?

4. What ultimate hope does verse 14 give us and those who wrestle with porn?

Hebrews 12:1–2; 10:24; 3:12–13

1. What new thing does Hebrews 12:1–2, 10:24, and 3:12–13 add to our discussion? (Hint: Does fighting sin happen only as an individual?) What role does this new thing play in the life of a believer? Explain.

2. Why might "looking to Jesus, the founder and perfecter of our faith" help us in running this race "with endurance"? How can we look to and trust in Jesus today in practical ways?

THE POINT

Summarize in your own words one point from this week's lesson.

WEEK FIVE:
MASTURBATION

THE SCENARIO

You are in biology class. The teacher is covering reproductive organs, and for some reason, she makes the off-handed remark, "You know what a great alternative to sex is? Masturbation." The class laughs, and the teacher moves on.

The rest of the scenario will be presented by your leader.

SCENARIO REFLECTIVE QUESTIONS

1. If the person in the scenario were raised in a Christian environment, why might he or she feel guilty or ashamed for masturbating?

2. Why might the person in the scenario be questioning the goodness of masturbation? What are some things that may or may not be good or healthy about masturbation? Explain.

3. Why do you think the person in the scenario even asks the question, "Could I stop if I wanted to?"

THE ISSUE: SONG OF SOLOMON 1:1–4; 3:1–2; 1 CORINTHIANS 6:17–20

Song of Solomon 1:1–4; 3:1–2

1. What do you think about the sexual desires that the woman in Song of Solomon has? Do you think they are godly or sinful? Explain.

2. What is the natural state of our sexual desires and our desires for pleasure? Who are they focused on? Explain.

3. Who is the focus of the woman in Song of Solomon 3:1–2? Does she just want the pleasure she can gain from the man? Explain.

4. How does your answer from question 3 affect how we think about masturbation?

1 Corinthians 6:17–20

1. First Corinthians 6:18 says, "Flee from sexual immorality." Paul gives multiple reasons for this in verses 17–20. Starting in verse 17, what do you think they are?

2. With the information given above, critique the statement, "Who cares if I masturbate or not? It's not harming anyone. I'm my own person!"

3. When someone chooses to pursue sexual faithfulness, what do you think are some common motivations for giving up masturbation? Compare and contrast these with the motivations Paul gives.

THE ISSUE IN LIFE: HEBREWS 4:15–16; HEBREWS 10:24–25

Hebrews 4:15–16

1. For students who feel the particular shame of masturbation, what hope can you offer from these verses? What's one way we can "draw near to the throne of grace"?

2. If we are thinking about the Triad of Life, what are some practical steps of faith and repentance a person who is struggling with masturbation can take?

Hebrews 10:24–25

1. Sexual sins turns us inward, to focus on ourselves. From Hebrews 10:24–25, what practical steps could someone who struggles with masturbation take to foster the aspect of love in the Triad of Life?

THE POINT

Summarize in your own words one point from this week's lesson.

WEEK SIX:
HOMOSEXUALITY

THE SCENARIO

Remember our story from Week Two? Sarah has always been interested in things that most other girls are not, like working on cars with her dad. She has tried to fit in with other girls, but so far, that is not working.

Throughout middle school, Sarah has also found a home on the soccer team and has continued to play into her first year of high school. Kim, an older girl on the team, has actually taken an interest in Sarah, helping her navigate the high school terrain. Then, a boy in Sarah's class asked her to the homecoming dance. The dance sparked some thoughts within Sarah. She started to realize that she feels attracted to other girls and even now seems to have strong feelings for Kim.

SCENARIO REFLECTIVE QUESTIONS

1. Let's enter into Sarah's experience. How do you think she feels being able to hang out with her dad and having a home on the soccer team?

2. This is a repeat question from Week One, but it is worth thinking about again. For Sarah, how might she be feeling by not fitting in with the other girls because of her attractions? How do you think her gifts play into her feelings?

3. If Sarah has never experienced these feelings before, how might she feel knowing that she might be attracted to Kim?

THE ISSUE: EPHESIANS 5:31–32; ROMANS 1:24–27; 28–32; 1 CORINTHIANS 10:13

1. What is our culture's understanding of homosexuality? Why do you think the culture thinks this way?

2. What are your own thoughts regarding homosexuality? Explain.

Ephesians 5:31–32

1. Now that we've considered the culture's thoughts and your own thoughts, let's look at God's thoughts. What is human marriage based on? How is the union that believers share with Christ like the marriage between husband and wife?

2. In light of your answer to question 1, do you think the differing genders are irrelevant or unimportant in marriage? Explain how this relates to the issue of homosexuality and the idea of Christ and his bride, the church.

Romans 1:24–27

1. Going verse by verse, explain this passage in your own words.

2. How does Romans 1:24–27 connect with the Tree Metaphor? From these verses, is homosexual desire and behavior just about what we do with our bodies? Explain.

Romans 1:28–32; 1 Corinthians 10:13

1. Can you see yourself in Romans 1:28–32? How? Considering Romans 1:28–32 and 1 Corinthians 10:13, how might these verses change the way you view someone who might struggle with same-sex attraction?

THE ISSUE IN LIFE: COLOSSIANS 3:1–10; 1 CORINTHIANS 6:9–11; ROMANS 12:4–8

Colossians 3:1–10

1. Going verse by verse, what does Colossians 3:1–4 tell us about our identity, and the identity of someone who struggles with same-sex attraction, in Christ? Explain using your own words.

2. Because of the Christian's radical, new identity in Jesus, what commands does Paul give in Colossians 3:1–8? If we, ourselves, struggle with same-sex attraction, how can we do these things practically?

1 Corinthians 6:9–11

1. The issue of identity is very important. What do each of these defining characteristics of a Christian mean in verse 11? What does this mean for someone who struggles with same-sex attraction?

Romans 12:4–8

1. What aspect of the Triad of Life (faith, repentance, and love) does Romans 12:4–8 talk about? What does this have to do with the same-sex attracted person?

2. Given the Triad of Life, what do you think is the goal of life for someone who is same-sex attracted? Is it heterosexuality? Explain.

THE POINT

Summarize in your own words one point from this week's lesson.

WEEK SEVEN:
TRANSGENDER

THE SCENARIO

Currently, there are a host of things associated with transgender. We live in a culture in which many people believe gender is fluid and nonbinary—meaning that "male" and "female" are not the only ways of being human. Transgenderism is a broad term that does not view gender as binary in nature (people being either male or female) but sees gender as a spectrum. The identity label "transgender" is adopted by individuals who reject the traditional view that personal identity is associated with biological sex. Under this category of transgender, there are also individuals who experience gender dysphoria; individuals who may adopt other pronouns not associated with their biological sex; others who see themselves as not having either a "male" or "female" gender based on their biology; those who seek to transition to the other gender using hormones or surgery; and others who, in a broad way, express or experience their gender in ways not aligned with their biological sex.

SCENARIO REFLECTIVE QUESTIONS

1. Explain what these terms mean: biological sex, gender, gender dysphoria, and transgender.

2. What do you think gender means?

3. Why do you think God created gender?

THE ISSUE: GENESIS 1:27; 2:18, 20–23; PSALM 139:13–18

1. One aspect of transgender is the experience of gender dysphoria. Which area of the Tree Metaphor do you think the experience of gender dysphoria most likely falls under? How does this change the way you might think of and approach gender dysphoria or a person who struggles with it?

2. Attempt to map out the Tree Metaphor in the contexts, desires, world-views, and behaviors for someone who expresses or experiences his or her "gender" in ways not aligned with biological sex.

Genesis 1:27; Genesis 2:18, 20–23; Psalm 139:13–18

1. What does Genesis 1:27 tell us about being created male or female? How does this change the way we view gender? Explain.

2. In Genesis 2:18, 20–23, who created gender and why? What difference does this make when we are thinking about issues of gender?

3. What does Psalm 139:13–16 tell us about being created male or female? How might the personal presence and creating role of God, especially verses 17–18, shape our thoughts of gender?

THE ISSUE IN LIFE: LUKE 9:21–24; JOHN 11:25–26; 1 CORINTHIANS 12:14–27

Luke 9:21–24; John 11:25–26

1. What does Luke 9:21–23 tell us about Christ and the Christian life in general?

2. What do these verses have to say to Christians who are struggling with their gender and its expression? What might this self-denying, cross-carrying aspect of the Christian life look like practically?

3. According to Luke 9:24 and John 11:25–26, what is our hope? What difference does that make to our sufferings now?

1 Corinthians 12:14–27

1. What are your general thoughts on this passage?

2. Remembering what we learned from Psalm 139, what does 1 Corinthians 12:14–27 say to individual Christians and to the gender-confused or gender-dysphoric student in particular?

3. What does this passage have to do with Christians as a group and those struggling with their gender? How does the fact that you are part of the body of Christ change the way you relate to a Christian struggling with his or her gender?

4. If someone we know comes to us and reveals that he or she is struggling with his or her gender, what might be some helpful responses?

THE POINT

Summarize in your own words one point from this week's lesson.

WEEK EIGHT:
DATING

THE SCENARIO

Jonathan is in ninth grade and has just asked out Emily. Jonathan and Emily's friends have boyfriends and girlfriends and are constantly telling them both about everything they're missing. But Jonathan and Emily are thinking differently. They are not simply dating to have a fun experience.

Recently, Jonathan committed his life to Christ and really wants to approach his relationship with Emily in a way that honors Christ. He also wants to honor her and protect both of them from the sexual mistakes he sees his peers making. He is really questioning, "How far is too far? How can we date in a godly way?" Similarly, Emily has been a Christian for years and really wants their relationship to honor God. She is also a little hesitant to date. She wonders, "What's the purpose of dating? What are our intentions?"

SCENARIO REFLECTIVE QUESTIONS

1. In what ways can you relate to Jonathan's or Emily's experience? In what ways is your experience different?

2. How would you answer, "How far is too far?"

THE ISSUE: MATTHEW 22:34–40

1. What is the world's concept of dating? What do you think the purpose of dating is? Explain.

2. How has Jesus fulfilled these two great commandments?

3. How do the Triad of Life (faith, repentance, and love) and Jesus's commandments challenge us to rethink dating and the question, "How far is too far?"

THE ISSUE IN LIFE: JOHN 15:12–13; 1 TIMOTHY 5:1–2; PROVERBS 7

John 15:12–13; 1 Timothy 5:1–2

1. John 15:12–13 points to Christ's sacrifice on behalf of his people. From this passage, what do you think one of the purposes of dating might be? Thinking about the Tree Metaphor, what desires (roots) and worldviews (trunk) would someone have to have if pursuing this purpose in dating?

2. Given Paul's commands in 1 Timothy 5:1–2, what is a basic way to view each other as fellow Christians? How does this view challenge us in dating? Explain.

3. In light of our discussion so far, what do you think about dating someone who does not believe in Christ?

4. How can we, practically and specifically, respond to Jesus's words and actions from John 15:12–13 while dating? Here is another way to think about this: What are some physical, emotional, and spiritual boundaries we may want to set up in dating?

Proverbs 7

1. What imagery is used in Proverbs 7:22–27 to describe the seduced man? How might this imagery apply to dating?

2. Can you see yourself in both roles here? In other words, do only women seduce? Are only men seduced? Explain. How should your answer change the way you date?

3. Translating Proverbs 7:6–9 into our modern context, what are some scenarios that might be similar to "passing along the street near her corner" or "taking the road to her house"? Be specific. At what point in the dating relationship do you think you should identify possible tempting situations for you and the person you are dating? Before or during? Why?

4. In light of our discussion on establishing boundaries, how would you feel doing this in your current (or future) relationship? What are some ways to begin setting up good boundaries to fulfill the two great commandments mentioned above? Explain.

5. Let's say that Jonathan and Emily will not end up getting married. What practical advice would you give them to help their story end well?

6. Thinking about all that we have talked about in the study until now, our new identity in Jesus, and the power that is within us by the Spirit, what are some things you would say to Jonathan and Emily if they had already crossed a sexual boundary? What can we assure them about God? What can we tell them about themselves? What advice might we give them in terms of dating?

THE POINT

Summarize in your own words one point from this week's lesson.

WEEK NINE:
SINGLENESS

THE SCENARIO

Katie's sister, Anna, is getting married. Katie sees how happy her sister is and thinks about how wonderful Anna's life will be now that she has found her husband. Anna is twenty-six, while Katie is only eighteen. But Katie has never dated, and there are no prospects on the horizon. Most of her friends have had multiple boyfriends and girlfriends. Some have even been dating for a couple of years. Finishing up high school and facing the prospect of indefinite singleness, she thinks, "Will I ever meet a guy who likes me?"

Chris, a friend of the family, looks on as Anna takes her vows. Chris has dated a few girls over the years, but as a sophomore in high school, he has already made some dating mistakes. Pornography and messing around sexually have played a big part in his high school career. But he wants to change. He wants to do things differently. But as he looks at the twenty-nine-year-old groom, the goal of staying sexually pure until marriage seems like an insurmountable challenge.

SCENARIO REFLECTIVE QUESTIONS

1. How might Katie feel as she looks in at her sister's wedding?

2. For Chris, why might "staying sexually pure until marriage" seem "like an insurmountable challenge"? Can you relate to Chris? Why or why not?

3. What are your views on singleness? What are some unique challenges that someone who is single either for an extended time in life or for all of life might face?

THE ISSUE: 1 CORINTHIANS 7:29–35

1. Imagine a single person, either single for life or for a season. Describe the different possible aspects of their Tree Metaphor (soil, roots, trunk, fruit).

2. What are some assumptions about single people that our culture or other Christians might have? What do you think about these assumptions? Explain.

3. In 1 Corinthians 7:29–35, how does Paul describe the single person and that person's life? How does Paul's understanding of the unmarried Christian life match up or differ from cultural stereotypes of singleness?

4. What are some expectations about singleness that you might have that Paul would not have?

5. Given Paul's words, how might single people, even as students, practically devote themselves in an undivided way to the Lord? How do we fight against the pressure to be always in a dating relationship? Explain.

6. Does question 3 change your view of the single life? Why or why not?

THE ISSUE IN LIFE: 1 THESSALONIANS 5:14; ROMANS 8:28–39

1. Let's think through the Triad of Life (faith, repentance, and love) and singleness. What does faith look like for the unmarried Christian? What are some specific things an unmarried Christian might have to repent of? How can an unmarried Christian love others and love God in specific ways?

1 Thessalonians 5:14

1. What does each verb (admonish, encourage, and help) in 1 Thessalonians 5:14 mean? In carrying out 1 Thessalonians 5:14, how might an unmarried high school student practice Christian community? Be specific.

Romans 8:28–39

1. What things might be hard to believe about Romans 8:28–39 given this discussion on singleness? How does Romans 8:28–39 speak both to Katie, who wonders if she will ever find the right guy, and to Chris, who wonders how he will stay sexually pure until marriage? How does Romans 8:28–39 speak into your situation?

THE POINT

Summarize in your own words one point from this week's lesson.

WEEK TEN:
MARRIAGE

THE SCENARIO

Christina and Matt are getting married. As they near the end of the service, their minister turns to Matt: "Will you, Matt, have this woman to be your wedded wife, to live with her after God's commandments in the holy state of marriage? And will you love her, honor and cherish her, so long as you both shall live?"

Matt responds, "I do," and then repeats after the minister: "I take you, Christina, to be my wedded wife, and I do promise and covenant, before God and these witnesses, to be your loving and faithful husband, in plenty and in want, in joy and in sorrow, in sickness and in health, as long as we both shall live."

SCENARIO REFLECTIVE QUESTIONS

1. What are your first impressions of the vows written above? What stands out to you? Is there anything you think is really good about them? Does anything seem weird?

2. What worldviews about God, others, and self would someone need to keep his or her commitment to the vows listed above?

3. Compare and contrast these vows with what you think most people in the culture think about marriage.

THE ISSUE: EPHESIANS 5:22–33; MATTHEW 22:30; REVELATION 19:6–9

Ephesians 5:22–33

1. What bigger story is human marriage supposed to tell? What specific details or aspects of this story is marriage supposed to display?

Matthew 22:30

1. What is the resurrection? How does that relate to marriage?

2. How might our Christian culture be shocked by Matthew 22:30? Explain.

Revelation 19:6–9

1. In light of Revelation 19:6–9 and Matthew 22:30, will there be marriage in heaven?

2. In verse 9, what does the Lamb have to do with the prophecy of Genesis 3:15 mentioned in Week Two, "I will put enmity between you and the woman, and between your offspring and her offspring; he shall bruise your head, and you shall bruise his heel"?

3. How did the Lamb love his bride? What does this have to do with Ephesians 5:25? How might this vision work out practically for husbands?

4. How does the "fine linen, bright and pure" and the "righteous deeds of the saints" in Revelation 19:8–9 relate to Ephesians 5:26–27? How does this shape your view of marriage?

THE ISSUE IN LIFE: PHILIPPIANS 2:1–13

1. What is the relationship between verses 1–5 and verses 6–11? Explain the verses and sections.

2. Practically, how might we do verses 1–4 in our families? How might we do verses 1–4 at school?

3. How does the normal Christian life of Philippians 2:1–11 relate to the married Christian life of Ephesians 5:22–33? How does this shape our understanding of marriage?

4. What does Philippians 2:1–11 indirectly say about faith and repentance?

5. How does the concept of working out our salvation (Philippians 2:12–13) relate to the holiness Christ produces in his church (Ephesians 5:26–27; Revelation 19:8–9)? Relate this to living sexually faithful lives, in light of our union with Christ.

THE POINT

Summarize in your own words one point from this week's lesson.

LEADER'S GUIDE

INTRODUCTION

Alive: Gospel Sexuality for Students is a ten-week, small group study that covers many of the major issues concerning human sexuality. Because God has placed students in our lives to love and disciple, we have the joy and privilege of being able to connect the grand truths of Jesus Christ to the everyday details of student life. Students, like all of us, are clamoring for a steadfastness and a hope in the world in which they live, and God has given us the opportunity to help students see that despite the sexual chaos of the world around us—and the chaos we experience in our own sexuality—Jesus is Lord and Savior.

THE VISION

Students can often feel as if the gospel has little relevance in day-to-day living. We long to help students see that the risen and ascended Lord makes all the difference in every area of our lives. This study seeks to unpack and apply the rich truths of the believers' union with Christ to the particulars of human sexuality. In other words, believers have died with Christ and now live with him, and by his Spirit, Christ provides both the motivation and power for believers to use their sexuality for his glory. Nothing, not even our sexuality, is outside his transforming work and power. Here is the vision from the apostle Paul:

> If then you have been raised with Christ, seek the things that are above, where Christ is, seated at the right hand of God. Set your minds on things that are above, not on things that are on earth. For you have died, and your life is hidden with Christ in God. When Christ who is your life appears, then you also will appear with him in glory. (Colossians 3:1–4)

The study aims to meet students where they are, talking about issues that are part of their everyday world. But we also want to lead them toward robust, deep, and strengthening theological content that will help them follow Jesus in the area of sexuality. As students hopefully identify with the content, our prayer is that they will be challenged to grow further in their Christian walk.

THE STUDY

We have designed this study to be used in a small group that is conversational and interactive but also guided by a leader. The ideal age group for this curriculum would be high school students, but with the right amount of wisdom, it can also be used as early as eighth grade and as late as college.

This study does not rely on lectures or extensive outside work for the students. To prepare to lead a group, we suggest that you review the material before each week so that you are familiar with the questions, suggested alternative questions, and content in the Leader's Guide. There is no homework for students to do outside of each week's lesson. However, you might suggest to students that they go over the next lesson a week in advance on their own and write down their thoughts.

Each week should focus mainly on discussion and application. *Alive: Gospel Sexuality for Students* is meant to be an inductive exploration. Instead of giving students a main point up front, students are encouraged to develop the main point of the lesson as the lesson itself progresses.

The nature of both students and the content of this study means that there will be times of awkward silence and intense floor staring. Do not be afraid to let those crickets chirp and to give students the time to process. Hopefully, through your relationships with your students and through the intentional time set aside to address these issues each week, conversation and discussion will flow more naturally as the study progresses.

Because of the content, this study will be best used in gender-specific, smaller group settings. If you decide to use this study in Sunday school, it is recommended that you divide the class into single-sex groups. Students can then build relationships with their leaders and their peers, and they will feel more comfortable talking about sexual issues without fearing the gaze of their opposite-gender peers.

EACH WEEK

Most weeks contain the elements listed below, though some do not. Here is a general outline of each lesson:

Every lesson takes about 45 minutes. Time limits are only suggestions, but do try to get through the lesson's content each week.

1. Lesson Goals

There are two to three lesson goals listed each week in the Leader's Guide, which form the backbone of each lesson. Use them as a template. We would like leaders to emphasize each of the goals for that week, even though they might spend more time on certain questions and points than others.

2. The Scenario

We begin each week with a scenario that sets up the main topic for that day. This scenario is meant to be a simple, quick way to break some of the tension and to introduce the issue at hand in a way that does not put students on the spot, hopefully creating a safer atmosphere to discuss it. After all, it is much easier to think about the sins and sufferings of someone else than it is to talk about one's own.

3. Scenario Reflective Questions *(5–7 minutes)*

Each week we give some reflective questions on the scenario. The purpose is threefold: to help students think critically about the issues, to help students connect the scenario to topics discussed in previous weeks, and to help students enter into the scenario themselves, connecting their own experiences with that of the person(s) in the scenario.

4. The Issue *(10–15 minutes)*

This is an opportunity for students to connect specific, sexual issues with biblical, Christ-centered truth. Students will read and discuss several Scripture passages.

5. The Issue in Life *(10–15 minutes)*

This section is very practical, helping students to think through how the Scriptures and Jesus interact with particular sexual issues in their own lives. The goal is for students to think through ways they can walk with Jesus as they wrestle with particular sins and sufferings in everyday life.

6. The Point *(3–5 minutes)*

This same question every week asks the students to think through the week's main point. This is, of course, the inductive part of the study: Students form into one thought what they got out of the week. Students will have multiple answers, and that is okay.

LEADER CUES

The Leader's Guide is simple to use. Content for leaders is in the back of this study guide. Each lesson includes leader cues. These leader cues are divided into two types. The first type is actual content leaders might say to steer the group. This content is set off with a >. We have included alternate questions to ask as well. The second type of leader cues consist of content leaders might think about as they lead. These cues are meant to guide leaders, and they are *italicized*.

One thing to keep in mind: There is a lot of content to cover each week. Expect students' answers to vary in depth and length. This is why there are many questions to choose from in every lesson. Sometimes, there are multiple questions stacked on top of one another. Feel free to pick and choose which ones will be most helpful.

Do not feel pressured to cover all of the leader cues, and feel free to summarize certain points or questions to move through the lesson at a comfortable pace. We want leaders to progress through each week's content, even if it means editing on the fly and/or moving quickly through certain portions.

KEY TRUTHS AND CONCEPTS

This study is based on certain key, biblical truths that guide our discussion of the gospel and sexuality. There is also a glossary in the back to further reinforce these truths. Spend some time familiarizing yourself with these concepts.

Key Biblical Truths

1. The Human Heart

In the Bible, it is the human heart that defines people as individuals and is the mover of faith and trust. What goes on in people's hearts is what the Lord is most concerned with in their lives. It can even be thought of as their nature. What people's hearts desire and love leads to their thoughts and actions. Deuteronomy 6:5 says, "You shall love the LORD your God with all your heart and with all your soul and with all your might." Romans 10:10 says, "For with the heart one believes and is justified, and with the mouth one confesses and is saved."

Human hearts, naturally, have rejected God and have trusted in other things besides him for life and salvation. Beginning with Adam and Eve, people have rebelled against God. Their natural hearts are not neutral, or basically good, but are evil and corrupt (Genesis 8:21; Jeremiah 17:9). Not only are human hearts naturally evil, but the Bible even calls people "dead in" their "trespasses and sins" (Ephesians 2:1).

When people put their faith in Jesus, however, he makes them alive—new creations. Their hearts are radically transformed. The new nature of a believer is holy and clean (Ezekiel 36:26), although he or she will still struggle with sin on this side of eternity.

2. The New Creation

When people come to Jesus by faith, they become new creations (2 Corinthians 5:17). They are given the Spirit of God (Romans 8:9–11), who makes them alive in Christ (Ephesians 2:1–10). Believers are part of the new creation now, as they await the re-creation of all things in the future (Revelation 21—22).

3. Union with Christ

This might be the most important concept of this study. The reason why believers are new creations in Christ is because Jesus Christ was raised from the dead, the "first fruits" of new creation (Romans 6:4; 1 Corinthians 15:20). He has passed through death into a new, transformed, imperishable life. Christians are united to Christ by the Spirit; their identity with the old creation and with Adam is broken as they share in Christ's death, and they are raised to new life with him (Colossians 3:1–4). Christians have a resurrected life in Christ now (Romans 6:1–4), and they will be resurrected in glory when he comes again (1 Corinthians 15). Christians are seated with Christ now (Ephesians 2:6), and they will reign with him for eternity. This can be put into a simple saying: So goes Christ, so go all who put their faith in him. As Paul said, "I have been crucified with Christ. It is no longer I who live, but Christ who lives in me. And the life I now live in the flesh I live by faith in the Son of God, who loved me and gave himself for me" (Galatians 2:20).

Because of what Christ has done for his people, and who they are in him, believers have undergone a fundamental identity shift from sinner to saint. Christians are brought back into relationship with God through Jesus (John 14:6). They are adopted as sons and daughters through the blood of Christ. He paid for their sins, and now they are fully forgiven (1 John 1:9; 4:10–11). They are set apart for him now and have peace with God for eternity (Romans 5:1), giving them total access to God as their Father (Romans 8:15–17).

4. Flesh and Spirit

Within believers, there remains something of the "flesh" (their old desires, their old sin patterns). Paul explains, "the desires of the flesh are against the Spirit, and the desires of the Spirit are against the flesh, for these are opposed to each other, to keep you from doing the things you want to do" (Galatians 5:17). But the flesh does not define a believer like it does an unbeliever. The Holy Spirit in the believer will have the upper hand and will complete the work that God started (Philippians 1:6).

Key Concepts

1. The Tree Metaphor

The Scriptures give us many places to go to understand people. In Luke 6:43–45, Jesus gives a helpful metaphor about people, where the most fundamental part of who they are is the heart, or seed of the tree.

We can expand Jesus's metaphor to take into account other aspects of human existence as well. The tree's seed is planted in soil that it cannot control. In the same way, people live in contexts they cannot always control—and these correspond to the sufferings, hardships, and general things people can't control in life.

From people's hearts flow their desires (James 1:14–15). These can easily correspond to the roots of the tree. People seek to be nourished and fed through what they desire, just as roots seek out nutrients.

People's hearts, the context in which they live, and their desires ultimately form their worldview, corresponding to the tree's trunk. The trunk of the tree holds the tree up. In the same way, people's worldviews about God, themselves, and others hold them up and transform the way they live (Romans 1:22–25). People's behavior (the fruit) flows directly from their worldviews. What people really think about God, themselves, and other people always produces their actions and behaviors.

2. The Triad of Life

The Triad of Life is the way we live the Christian life. The Triad of Life consists of three things: faith, repentance, and love. When Jesus comes on to the scene, he says, "The time is fulfilled, and the kingdom of God is at hand; repent and believe in the gospel" (Mark 1:15). Repentance from sin and faith in Jesus are flip sides of the same coin. Both are required for people to be saved and transformed in Christ, and both are required every day in the lives of believers. Following from the first and second great commandments (Matthew 22:37–40), love for God and others forms the outward expression of the Christian life. Turning from sin and to Jesus in faith, as well as loving and serving God and others, characterize a believer's life.

One more thing before you jump in: The issues discussed in this study are extremely sensitive. Students will have baggage, fear, and shame when talking about them—as many, if not most, of them have already experienced firsthand what will be discussed. Therefore, it is important for you to offer yourselves continually as people whom students can trust. Students need to know they can count on us to show them the grace and love of Jesus, and that we are people who are committed to helping them and walking alongside of them.

We recommend that each week you emphasize your care for your students. Praying before and after your time together can help students see their God is someone who cares deeply about the issues discussed and their leaders are dependent upon him to move and work.

We pray that as you and your students discuss these issues, Christ will become more and more beautiful to everyone, and that your students' desire to follow him with their sexuality will increase every week. May the good news of Christ—that he has come to make new what was broken, to give life where there was death, to offer forgiveness and grace where there is sin, and to transform sinners into people who treasure him above all—become our sole hope as we journey forward.

> Now may the God of peace who brought again from the dead our Lord Jesus, the great shepherd of the sheep, by the blood of the eternal covenant, equip you with everything good that you may do his will, working in us that which is pleasing in his sight, through Jesus Christ, to whom be glory forever and ever. Amen.
>
> Hebrews 13:20–21

WEEK ONE:
WHAT DOES GOD HAVE TO DO
WITH SEXUALITY?

> LESSON GOALS

1. Explore the basic ideas of sexuality, marriage, and covenant.
2. Explore the truth that God created our sexuality and the implications of that in our lives.

These first three weeks will be different than the weeks to come, as they lay a broad foundation for understanding our sexuality and the complexity we experience as human beings. First, to understand our sexuality and what went wrong, we have to understand where it all began.

PRAY

THE SCENARIO *(Have a student read this aloud.)*

> Then the man said, "This at last is bone of my bones and flesh of my flesh; she shall be called Woman, because she was taken out of Man." Therefore a man shall leave his father and his mother and hold fast to his wife, and they shall become one flesh. And the man and his wife were both naked and were not ashamed. (Genesis 2:23–25)

SCENARIO REFLECTIVE QUESTIONS *(10 minutes)*

1. Genesis 2:24 is the first mention of marriage in the Bible. Christians refer to this as the "covenant" of marriage. What might be the difference between a covenant and two people who make a commitment to live together? Which is safer, covenant or commitment? Why?

> *Brainstorm with students the difference between marriage (a legally binding covenant) and making a commitment to live with someone. Christians refer to marriage as a covenant because it is more than commitment.* A covenant is a binding obligation between a man and woman, before God and others, that ultimately requires each individual to love and serve, regardless of how one is feeling. A marriage covenant is a legally binding act, in God's kingdom and in the world's eyes, that sets the duties of love before each partner.

A commitment is less safe than a covenant because a commitment is not necessarily legally binding and can be tossed aside when someone feels as if he or she does not want to be committed anymore. *Be aware students might think a commitment to living together would be safer because you would possibly avoid the hurt and distress of divorce. But the avoidance of hurt does not necessarily make someone safe.*

Ultimately, the covenant of marriage provides the safety for individuals to be loved and served despite their own sin. The covenant means that, although each partner will sin against each other and fail, each partner is safe from abandonment—even if one spouse is simply unhappy or disillusioned.

2. In the covenant relationship, "the man and his wife were both naked and were not ashamed." What does this tell you about life in the garden?

> God made the garden as a safe place for Adam and Eve to be exposed to each other. The garden was a place where Adam and Eve were free from fear, free from shame, and free from death.

THE ISSUE *(10 minutes)*: GENESIS 1:26–31; 2:15–17

Have someone read Genesis 1:26–31; 2:15–17.

1. Before God creates the covenant of marriage, what does God create in Genesis 1:26–27? What difference does it make to sexuality that God himself created, and created things "very good" in verse 31?

> God creates en-gendered people—i.e., people with genders. Humanity does not exist to decide gender: God creates it. He also creates the two genders each bearing separately and together the image of God.

Gender is not something to be sculpted depending on people's desires or to be seen as irrelevant to our lives. Gender is meant to be embraced and celebrated. In fact, our gender is "very good."

2. In Genesis 1:28, were sex or our sexuality created for a purpose or as an end in themselves? Explain.

> Our sex and sexuality were created for a purpose. Sex is meant for pleasure but was also intended to create children. We were meant to use our sexuality in ways that extend the image of God over creation as we reign and rule in God's name. Thus, the coming together of two separate genders, in some way, reflects God's image as they reign and rule over creation.

3. What does Genesis 1:29–30 tell you about the character of God? What does God's character have to do with sex and sexuality?

> God gives good things to his children. He gives them "every plant yielding seed" and "every tree with seed in its fruit" to have for food. God is not a God who is removed from his creation or who does not care for his creation. He is a loving God who provides.

Our sexuality was meant for our good and comes from the goodness of God. God's good character means he does not create anything that is evil.

4. What is a worldview? How might Adam and Eve have viewed each other, God, and the world around them given Genesis 1:26–31?

> A worldview is a way people interpret life, all of life—everything that happens to them, around them, or far away from them. A worldview is like a pair of glasses through which people see and interpret everything in the world. Everyone wears a pair of world-view glasses. A worldview is an outlook on God, oneself, and others

that directly shapes people's actions. In other words, what people think about God, what they think about themselves, and what they think about other people directly influence the things they do.

In the garden, before sin, Adam and Eve loved and worshipped God. Adam viewed Eve as someone to be treasured, "This at last is bone of my bones and flesh of my flesh" (Genesis 2:23). Eve was given to Adam as his equal and perfect-fitting companion, someone who would work alongside him as they both stewarded God's creation. Eve, in return, viewed Adam as someone to be helped and supported. They viewed the world around them through the lens of God: It was his creation, but they were creation's stewards. They were meant to take care of what God had created (Genesis 1:26–28). That was their original worldview.

5. What does Genesis 2:15–17 tell us about the original relationship between Adam and God?

> The relationship God establishes with Adam is a covenant relationship. It is a binding obligation with both blessings and curses. It is important to note that, before telling Adam what he cannot do, God tells Adam what he has done to provide for Adam, "You may surely eat of every tree of the garden." God's relationship with Adam is loving from the beginning; God extends his love, care, and provision to Adam from the start.

THE ISSUE IN LIFE (15–20 minutes)

1. According to our culture, how do Christians view sex and sexuality? Looking back at question 3 in "The Issue," how does God's Word present sex and sexuality? Compare and contrast God's voice and our culture's voice on sex and sexuality.

> The world tends to view Christians and their thoughts on sex and sexuality as backward, outdated, and repressed, meaning that we are suppressing natural, good desires by limiting sex to the covenant of marriage. Many think that Christians devalue women and promote male superiority.

The truth is that Christians celebrate our sex and sexuality. God is the most pro-sex being in the universe. We also view each gender with dignity and respect. Each one bears the image of God. This means both men and women have inherent dignity and should be treated with love and respect.

2. Do you normally think about sex and sexuality with God in the mix? Explain.

3. What can we expect from life since God created human beings with sexual desire? Explain.

> At this point, we have not introduced the concept of the Fall, but we can still see that, as human beings, we have God-given sexual desires. This means that life is going to be filled with sexual tension, frustration, and desire. We can expect the desire to feel intimate with another human being. We should expect to want to feel good and experience pleasure.

4. Practically, how can Christians live godly lives in light of their God-given sexual desires and sexuality?

> We can recognize that our sexual desires are gifts from God and function under God. They are not something evil in and of themselves, but they are not something to be obeyed if they go against our Maker. In other words, we must also fight against the urge to satisfy our sexual desires in ways that do not honor God.

As we have seen in this lesson, our sexuality and the fact that each one of us has a gender that bears the image of God means that we should work hard to value, treasure, and love others. *Have your students think about what it means to value and love parents, siblings, and friends who all share the image of God in tangible, practical ways.*

THE POINT *(3–5 minutes)*

Summarize, in your own words, one point from this week's lesson.

Give your students time to think, and let multiple students answer.

PRAY

WEEK TWO:
WHAT WENT WRONG?

> LESSON GOALS

1. Explore various topics of sexual brokenness.
2. Explore the Fall and how it relates to our sexuality.
3. Explore how Jesus saves us and works in us the Triad of Life.

PRAY

THE SCENARIO *(Have a student read this aloud.)*

Sam and Heather have been dating for a few months. Sam is pressuring Heather to go further physically in their relationship, saying things like, "Look. It's no big deal. Don't you want to take our relationship to the next level?"

Sarah has been feeling differently for years now. She has tried to get into the things that interest other girls, but she just cannot. She feels more at home with her dad and fixing cars, but she also listens, time and again, to her friends talk about their boyfriends and has started to pick up on something else. She feels attracted to other girls.

Mike rushes home every day. He is a loner with not many friends, much less a girlfriend. He anticipates his afternoons and thinks about them throughout his day, and finally, when school gets out, he longs to get home and into his room. As he sits alone, day after day, he views countless pornographic videos and images.

SCENARIO REFLECTIVE QUESTIONS *(10 minutes)*

1. Let's think through the scenarios above. For Sam and Heather, why do you think Sam wants to go further physically? What are some desires he might have? How might Heather feel? What might be some of her desires?

> Possibly, Sam wants to push things physically because he simply wants to feel good. Maybe Sam wants to live up to his friends' expectations and experiences, believing that "everyone is doing it." He might simply desire Heather sexually.

Alternate Questions

1. If you were in either Sam's or Heather's shoes, how might you be feeling?

2. How might you feel if someone you were dating pressured you to do things that made you uncomfortable?

Heather's feelings could be very conflicted. She might really love her relationship with Sam, but she might not be willing to take these next steps with him. Heather might feel scared that if she does not do what he wants, their relationship would end. She also might feel the pressure from a culture that says, "There's nothing wrong with this, as long as you aren't hurting anyone." Heather could really desire closeness with Sam but maybe not sexual closeness. Now that Sam is pushing sexual intimacy, she might also really desire to get out of the relationship.

2. For Sarah, how might she feel about not fitting in with the other girls? What things play into her feelings of not fitting in? Explain.

Alternate Question

1. How would you feel if you did not fit in with your friend group?

> Sarah might feel like an outsider, like she simply does not belong. She might also feel frustrated that she does not belong and wants to grasp onto anything that will make her feel like a "normal" girl. Sarah is clearly gifted and is passionate about things like sports, but her attraction toward other girls also isolates her from the "boy talk" that her friends share.

3. In light of using porn, how might Mike feel about himself? How might he feel about the world around him? How might he feel about others, especially girls?

> For Mike, pornography is something he can manipulate to, among other things, alleviate his feelings of loneliness: Every day he knows he can go home, and porn will be waiting for him. All he has to do is open up his device, and there it is. Mike might feel like there is so much in his life he cannot control, like his lack of friends or romantic relationships. He may also feel that it is up to him to make himself happy, since no one else is looking to meet his needs for intimacy and safety. Mike might also view the world around him as something to be taken control of, to be used by him for his own ends because, right now, life feels out of his control. This mind-set of using the world around him affects how he views other people, especially girls. He feels like he can use the images of these girls to make himself feel better.

THE ISSUE *(30 minutes)*: GENESIS 1:27–28; 3:1–24; JOHN 14:6; MARK 1: 14–15; MATTHEW 22: 36–40

Genesis 1:27–28

Have someone read Genesis 1:27–28.

1. How does the world think gender and sexual identity are formed? Why is it significant that God creates and has a specific design for these things?

> **Alternate Question**
>
> 1. How might someone in your school view gender and sexuality?

> The world tells us that gender and marriage are cultural constructs, and individuals determine their own sexual identity and sexual behaviors as long as no one is harmed in the process.

God, not culture or any individual, creates gender and sexuality. Because they are his creations, he—and only he—has the right to determine truth about them. God is the authority over gender, marriage, and sexuality. This also means that it is our duty, as God's creations, to make sure we are living according to his designs. We are most free when we are living within his designs. This really does bring up the question: Who is calling the shots in your life?

Genesis 3:1–6

Have someone read Genesis 3:1–6.

1. What do you think it means that the serpent "was more crafty than any other beast of the field that the LORD God had made"? What were the serpent's tactics in tempting Eve?

> The serpent's interaction with Eve is subtle and deceitful without being, at least at first, overtly sinister, though his overtness comes out at as the conversation progresses. First, Satan starts a conversation with Eve that sows seeds of doubt concerning God. He even twists God's words. Second, the serpent flat-out tells Eve a lie. Third, Satan makes it seem as if God is holding out on Eve—that God actually does not want, and has not given, the best for Eve.

2. Thinking specifically about the scenario situations, how does sexual temptation make us doubt God and his intentions for us? What things might sexual temptation tell us about God's motives and character? Have you ever felt these tactics in action? Explain.

| **Alternate Question** |
| 1. Does sexual sin often start out as blatantly evil? Explain. |

> Heather might feel very insecure around Sam, thinking that all other girls do sexual things with their boyfriends; out of her insecurity, she feels as if she must go further with him. Sam, on the other hand, might feel as if the best life is not to be lived in accordance with God's ways. He feels he must act now sexually or miss out. In the case of Sarah, the temptation might be to define herself as gay, because she believes that God simply made her this way; the best life to be lived would be in obedience to her desires. For Mike,

he might be tempted to view God as distant and not able to help him, as if God did not care about him or his suffering.

Sexual temptation often makes it seem as if we are missing out on crucial aspects of life, whether it be actual sex or a robust fantasy life. In other words, at its core, sexual temptation questions God's motives and character. It really does begin as a conversation in our mind, as we question God himself. As it progresses, and we sin, we come to believe that sin gives us the good things that God has withheld.

Genesis 3:7–13

Have someone read Genesis 3:7–13.

1. In light of Adam's and Eve's rebellion, shame comes into the picture. What is shame? What does shame have to do with Adam's and Eve's hiding? What does shame have to do with sexual sin?

> **Alternate Questions**
> 1. What does it feel like when you make a mistake and everyone is watching you?
> 2. What do you want to do in that situation?

> Think about Genesis 2:25 and contrast it with Genesis 3:7. Shame often includes the fear of what other people think about us and can be experienced like a prison of other people's condemning gazes. Shame makes people want to hide, because they might feel like outsiders. They feel alone and completely different, without true companionship. Because of shame, Adam and Eve try and hide themselves from each other.

Individuals who struggle with sexual sin can feel dirty, stained, different, and distant from the rest of humanity, thinking that they are the only ones who have messed up.

2. As well as shame, the concept of fear is introduced here. What is fear? What does

> **Alternate Question**
> 1. How is fear different than shame?

that have to do with Adam's and Eve's hiding? What does fear have to do with sexual sin?

> Fear has to do with consequences and guilt. We feel guilty, and we fear what may result from our sin. Because Adam and Eve felt other and alien, because they felt ashamed, and knew that they had sinned, they hid themselves from God, fearing his judgment and wrath. In a similar way, sexual sin can produce massive amounts of fear, isolation, and secrecy, as we often do not want to own up to our own sin, what our sin does, and what our sin merits.

Genesis 3:14–19

Have someone read Genesis 3:14–19.

1. In response to Adam's and Eve's rebellion, God curses them. What are the curses that God gives to Adam and Eve? What does this mean for humanity now?

Alternate Questions

1. In what ways do you see the Fall at work in the world generally?
2. In what ways do you see the Fall at work in the world sexually?

> Broadly, people's relationships are broken, and our time on this earth is characterized by hardship and suffering.

2. What hope does God offer Adam and Eve? Why does this do away with man's fear and shame in relationship to God?

> Spend some time with students considering verse 15. Ultimately, verse 15 means that there is war between the offspring of the woman, that is, all of humanity, and the offspring of the serpent, that is, all evil and godlessness in the world.

Alternate Questions

1. What does it mean that there will be enmity between the woman and the serpent?
2. Why do you think these verses single out an offspring of the woman who will bruise the head of the serpent?
3. What do you think it means that the serpent will bruise the offspring's heel?

Verse 15 points to Christ, who is both God and man, who will deliver the deathblow to Satan by his life, death, and resurrection. It points both to the suffering Christ experienced on behalf of his people and his ultimate victory over evil. God will finally win the day.

God will finally pour out his anger and wrath on Christ instead of his people. God sent Jesus because he loves his people, and he also sent Jesus to take his people's place on the cross. In Christ, men and women do not need to fear God's anger and wrath any longer.

Genesis 3:20–24

Have someone read Genesis 3:20–24.

1. Despite the curses God gives, God covers Adam and Eve. What does this act have to do with shame (read 2 Corinthians 5:21)? What does this act reveal about God's character?

> He is a gracious God who works to remove Adam's and Eve's shame and fear. Shame can feel like stained clothing, yet God gives Adam and Eve more dignified clothing, a sign pointing to the complete righteousness he will offer as clothing in and through Jesus. God does not only respond in judgment, but he acts as a Father who loves and is faithful to his children. Some even see the fact that God spills the blood of animals, using their skin to cover Adam and Eve, as pointing forward to how God requires a sacrifice in humanity's place for their sins. Christ fulfills this principle as well.

In Christ, God credits the righteousness of Christ to us who believe in him, so that in him "we might become the righteousness of God" (2 Corinthians 5:21). In Christ, God sees his people as righteous instead of as sinful. Shame and fear are done away with; we are clothed in Christ's perfect righteousness. God's wrath has been satisfied by Christ.

2. Why does God prevent Adam and Eve
from eating from the Tree of Life? What does
this reveal about God's character and plan?

Alternate Question

1. Why would it be a
   bad idea for Adam
   and Eve to live
   forever in the fallen
   state in which they
   are in?

> God does not allow Adam and Eve
to eat from the Tree of Life because he
knows that if they do, they will live forever in the state of the curse.

This reveals that God does care about his creation and has a
plan to undo the evil that they caused.

John 14:6

Have someone read John 14:6.

1. Moving from Genesis to Jesus, what do you think it means for Jesus to
be "the way, and the truth, and the life"?

> It might be helpful to break this phrase down. First, what does
it mean for Jesus to be "the way"? Like Jesus says, there is no other
path to true relationship with God but through him. Jesus takes on
himself the judgment believers deserve and then credits his righteousness to them. This makes us acceptable in the sight of God
and enables us to be in relationship with him.

Next, what does it mean for Jesus to be "the truth"? It means
that he is the embodiment of truth. We take our cues from him,
and anything who opposes him is, by default, false and sinful. He
is right in everything he teaches and does.

Finally, what does it mean for Jesus to be "the life"? True life—
life that begins now and continues into eternity—is to be found
only in him. By trusting Jesus, believers will live forever. Life is to
be found by turning from our sin and trusting in Jesus, living lives
that love God and love others in light of his love for us. It also
means, as the apostle Paul said, "I have been crucified with Christ.
It is no longer I who live, but Christ who lives in me. And the life
I now live I live by faith in the Son of God, who loved me and

gave Himself for me" (Galatians 2:20). This means that our union with Christ involves new life, coming from him to us through the Holy Spirit.

2. Contrast Jesus's words in John 14:6 with the serpent's words in Genesis 3:1–5. What does this have to do with our sexuality?

> The serpent in the garden told Eve the way to true life was to follow her own desires. The serpent said God was, in fact, a liar, and that truth was to be found apart from God. We see where that line of thinking got us—the serpent offered a life that was actually death and slavery to sin.

In contrast to the serpent, we see that our sexuality is to be used in ways that are directed by God, in ways that are good for us and pleasing to him. As opposed to the serpent, we can trust God even though life is hard. In other words, to be a true man or woman of God is to trust in Christ first and foremost, knowing and believing that he is, in fact, "the way, and the truth, and the life" (John 14:6).

Mark 1:14–15; Matthew 22:36–40

Have someone read Mark 1:14–15 and Matthew 22:36–40.

1. Mark 1:14–15 and Matthew 22:36–40 form what we call the Triad of Life: The Christian life is to be lived in faith (trusting in Christ as Savior), repentance (turning from sin and turning to God in faith), and love (loving God and others). Given man's rebellion against God and God's pursuit of man in Christ, how does sexual sin distort and ruin faith and repentance?

> Mark 1:14–15 introduces the principles of faith and repentance. Our sexuality is corrupted by sin, making us selfish and rebellious, hating the ways of God. Sexual temptation begs us to trust in ourselves; it makes repentance (turning from sin and turning to Jesus) obsolete. To follow Christ, we must turn (or repent) from our pride and sin and turn to Christ. We must give up our own

thoughts about sex and sexuality and submit ourselves to God and his leadership.

This means turning away from things like pornography, lust, fantasy, and acting out sexually. It might even mean giving up certain relationships or technology. We must also put our faith in Christ daily. This means not only must we turn from our sin but we must every day also trust Christ, who he is, and what he has done for us. Repentance and faith are like two sides of the same coin: one comes with the other.

2. How does sexual sin destroy true love?

> The last piece of the Triad of Life, found in Matthew 22:36–40, is love.

Alternate Question
1. What are some tangible, real-life ways we can love others in our lives?

Faith and repentance always result in love for God and others. Sexual sin is inherently selfish and naturally uses and abuses others, treating them as objects. Sexual sin breaks down love toward God and neighbor. Temptation entices us not to serve and love others in light of Jesus but to use others for our own ends. It might seem out of the blue, but one of the most foundational ways we use our sexuality to God's glory and one of the greatest ways to fight sexual sin is by loving God and others. Loving God and others in practical ways moves us from sacrificing others for our own use to sacrificing ourselves for the benefit of others. This includes things like praying for one another, reading the Bible, and serving our family and friends in tangible, real-life ways. It is the move from treating others like objects to humanizing them and treating them with dignity.

THE POINT (3–5 minutes)

Summarize, in your own words, one point from this week's lesson.

Give your students time to think, and let multiple students answer.

PRAY

WEEK THREE:
THE TREE METAPHOR

> LESSON GOALS

1. Explore the Tree Metaphor and how it informs our sexuality.
2. Explore how the Fall has affected the Tree Metaphor.
3. Explore how Jesus transforms the Tree Metaphor.

PRAY

> *Leaders, this is going to be a hard week. The content is mostly conceptual, but it is crucial for students to understand the complexities that factor into sexual expression and behavior. It might be helpful for you to study this week thoroughly before helping your students walk through it.*

THE SCENARIO *(Have a student read this aloud.)*

The Tree Metaphor will be applied to last week's scenario. Even though it is the same content, we suggest having students reread the scenario out loud. There will be intentional overlap between the scenario questions asked last week and the Tree Metaphor this week, to further develop these categories.

In a youth group much like yours . . . Sam and Heather have been dating for a few months. Sam is pressuring Heather to go further physically in their relationship, saying things like, "Look. It's no big deal. Don't you want to take our relationship to the next level?"

Sarah has been feeling differently for years now. She has tried to get into the things that interest other girls, but she just cannot. She feels more at home with her dad and fixing cars, but she also listens, time and again, to her friends talk about their boyfriends and has started to pick up on something else. She feels attracted to other girls.

Mike rushes home every day. He is a loner with not many friends, much less a girlfriend. He anticipates his afternoons and thinks about them throughout his day, and finally, when school gets out, he longs to get home and into his room. As he sits alone, day after day, he views countless pornographic videos and images.

SCENARIO REFLECTIVE QUESTIONS *(10 minutes)*

Because there is a lot of content to get through, we will jump right into the Tree Metaphor itself.

An understanding of the human person comes from a variety of places in the Scriptures. In Luke 6:43–45, Jesus gives a helpful metaphor about people, where the most fundamental part of who they are is the heart, or seed of the tree.

The tree's seed is planted in soil that it cannot control. In the same way, people live in contexts they cannot always control, including the sufferings and hardships they experience in life.

From people's hearts flow their desires (James 1:14–15). These are the roots of the tree. People's desires are seeking nourishment from things around them. Just as roots seek soil full of nutrients, people desire and reach out for whatever they think might satisfy and/or save them.

People's hearts, the context in which they live, and their desires help to form their worldview, which corresponds to the tree's trunk. The trunk of the tree holds the tree up; in the same way, people's worldviews about God, themselves, and others hold them up and transform the way they live (Romans 1:22–25). People's behavior (the fruit) flows from their worldviews. What people really think about God, themselves, and other people produces their actions and behaviors.

> This week, we are going to be thinking about our sexuality and how complex it is. Hopefully, we can all walk away with a better sense of why we do the things we do.

THE ISSUE *(30 minutes)*: LUKE 6:43–45; ROMANS 10:10; PROVERBS 27:19; 2 CORINTHIANS 5:17; ECCLESIASTES 2:22–23; MATTHEW 16:24; JAMES 1:14–15; GALATIANS 5:16–17; ROMANS 1:22–25

Applying the Tree Metaphor

Luke 6:43–45; Romans 10:10

Have someone read Luke 6:43–45 and Romans 10:10.

1. If you had to apply the Tree Metaphor to Sam and Heather's situation, what is the sinful fruit?

> The fruit can be a couple of things: It can be the uncontrolled making out. It can be Sam pressuring Heather. It could be Heather's giving in. The fruit is any sinful, sexual behavior.

2. According to Romans 10:10 and beginning with the "seed" of the tree, why is Christ so concerned with our hearts? What do faith and trust have to do with sexual sin?

> Christ is concerned with our hearts because our hearts are the movers of faith and trust; the heart determines where we look for true life, true meaning, true purpose, and true salvation. This means that our sexual behavior has more to do with where we place our trust, whether we are pursuing Jesus, and what we believe than what we are doing with our bodies. This is one part of the Triad of Life: faith.

The Issue of Identity

Proverbs 27:19; 2 Corinthians 5:17

Have someone read Proverbs 27:19 and 2 Corinthians 5:17.

1. What are some things Proverbs 27:19 tells us about the heart, the seed of the human tree? How does the heart act as a reflective mirror? Explain.

> The heart reflects people's true nature: our identity. The heart is what defines us.

<table>
<tr><td>

Alternate Questions

1. What do you see reflected when you look straight down into water?

2. What does the Fall tell us about our hearts naturally?
</td></tr>
</table>

The Fall, of course, shows that we are all, naturally, sinners. We are not basically good or even morally neutral. *This is extremely important: our students must understand that ultimately, there are two, and only two, identities humans may have. They may either be defined by their sin, and thus as sinners, or [move on to the next question].*

2. What does 2 Corinthians 5:17 have to do with our hearts?

> If we come to Christ and trust in him with our lives, banking on him as Savior and Lord, then he radically transforms us. This transformation starts with our hearts. We have a new nature that defines us. We are new creations! Therefore, individuals fit into two ultimate identity categories: someone is either "in Christ" or "not in Christ." People are either identified as Christian with a new nature, or non-Christian with the old nature.

3. What do the terms "in Christ" and "new creation" in 1 Corinthians 5:17 have to do with sexual sin and identity? If a believer sins, does that mean he or she is not a Christian? Can the believer ever be ultimately defined by his or her sin? Explain.

> Sexual sin in the life of a believer does not mean that the believer is not a Christian. There remains in the life of a believer what the Scriptures call "the flesh" (Galatians 5:16–17; this is examined below)—which "wages war" against the Spirit in the believer. Sexual sin can never define a believer: A believer's identity is wrapped up in Christ and can never be ripped away. Second Corinthians 5:17 says that Christ, and the newness that he brings, is the most basic identity of every Christian. Our lives are wrapped in Jesus's resurrected life, meaning that what ultimately characterizes believers is new life and creation in Christ.

Ecclesiastes 2:22–23; Matthew 16:24

Have someone read Ecclesiastes 2:22–23; Matthew 16:24.

1. Moving on to the soil of the tree, what do you think is the point of Ecclesiastes 2:22–23?

> Life is full of suffering that we cannot control. Our daily life is characterized by difficulty, frustrations, and many times sorrow.

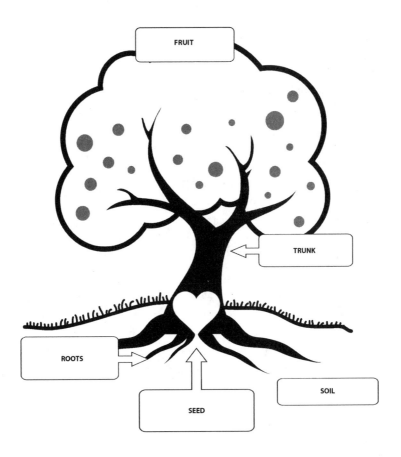

2. What are some specific things that have happened to you because you live in a fallen world? How is the soil of a tree like the sufferings we experience in life? What are some other sufferings Christians might face?

> **Alternate Question**
> 1. Can the seed of a tree choose what soil it is planted in? Do we get to choose the things that just happen to us? Explain.

> The soil ultimately corresponds to the things that we cannot control in life: physical characteristics, gift-sets, personality, feelings, family, our culture, socioeconomic status, abuse, spiritual warfare, death, sickness, the bodies we have, etc.

3. According to Matthew 16:24, what can the Christian expect from a life of following Christ? How does this match up to the category of the soil? Explain.

> A Christian can expect suffering and hardship, i.e., a cross to carry. There was life and resurrection for Jesus on the other side, however! Jesus promises his followers the same thing: As we follow him, we will have to die to ourselves, saying no to selfishness and to sinful desires and behaviors. However, we will find life in him both now and forever. We can also look forward to a physical resurrection from the dead to live with Christ forever.

Many times, Jesus's followers do not choose their crosses; many times, we often have no say in the matter. But our crosses and sufferings help us turn again and again to Christ. It might be helpful, as well, to get students to think about temptation: in the life of a believer, temptation can be a form of suffering with the world, our own sinful tendencies, and the devil against the new man. But these temptations drive us to Jesus, "For because he himself has suffered when tempted, he is able to help those who are being tempted" (Hebrews 2:18).

4. What are some sufferings that might be in play with Sarah?

> Sarah might feel like an outsider because of her gifts and attractions, like she simply does not belong. She did not necessarily

choose her gifts; the isolation she feels from not having similar gifts to the other girls could be part of her sufferings. She might also feel frustrated that she does not belong and wants to grasp onto anything that will make her feel like a normal girl.

James 1:14–15; Galatians 5:16–17

Have someone read James 1:14–15 and Galatians 5:16–17.

Alternate Question
1. Where do our desires come from?

1. The roots of the tree are, by nature, searching for water and nourishment. The roots of a tree can correspond to our own desires. Connecting James 1:14–15 to what we have talked about so far, why are our natural desires not good or even neutral? What are some desires you can think of that would contribute to our sexuality? Explain.

This is an important question that the group needs to unpack. Read through this answer and familiarize yourself with the direction of the answer.

> People's desires ultimately come from our hearts, and our hearts determine the character of our desires. This means that naturally, all desires, even though they might seem innocent, are actually fallen and corrupted to one degree or another. Without a change of heart, our desires are not oriented around the worship of God, but they tempt us to worship ourselves or anything other than God. Anything we worship other than God is an idol.

   Any desire at all can contribute to using our sexuality in fallen ways and in God-honoring ways. We can have desires for comfort, pleasure, safety, companionship, worshipping God, etc., all of which can feed into how we act sexually.

2. According to Galatians 5:16–17, what spiritual dynamic is at work in the desires of a believer? What desires of both the flesh and the Spirit might be at work in both Sam and Heather?

> There is a war going on in the believer between the flesh and the Spirit. In terms of fleshly desires, Sam obviously wants to push things sexually with Heather. He also might even consider manipulating her for his own ends. If both Sam and Heather are believers, after their intense make-out sessions, both of them could feel as if they are not honoring the other. On the positive side, and in the Spirit, they might really desire to love and protect the other one from sin. They might also genuinely want to follow Christ but feel enslaved to their fleshly desires.

For Heather, her fleshly desires could include wanting to please Sam over wanting to please the Lord, wanting to feel validated as a woman, wanting emotional validation at all costs, or simply wanting the physical pleasure without following the Lord.

Romans 1:22–25

Have someone read Romans 1:22–25.

1. What does the trunk of a tree do for the tree? How do our worldviews about God, ourselves, and other people act like the trunk of a tree? Explain.

> The trunk holds up and gives structure to the tree and enables it to bear fruit. Ultimately, our worldviews hold us up. Worldviews are the pillars of our lives. In the same way, our worldviews of God, ourselves, and other people hold us up and determine any action we choose to take.

2. Thinking about the trunk of the tree, what are some broken worldviews about God, ourselves, and others that Romans 1 brings up?

> It might be helpful to walk through the passage verse by verse. The people of Romans 1 clearly see God with a lowercase "g." God is able to be traded for other things without much thought. He might be seen

Alternate Question

1. How might the people of Romans 1 view God, others, and themselves?

as withholding the best from us, a liar, or a killjoy. God might be seen as a tyrant or unloving, and thus as someone to be discarded on a whim. The people of Romans 1 also see others as people to be worshipped and needed. The people of Romans 1 also implicitly see themselves as ones who have the right to set the real God aside. These people have repositioned God as a creature and lifted themselves up to the creator position. They functionally view themselves as gods of their own lives.

3. For Mike, what are some worldviews about God, himself, and others that might be in play?

> For Mike, pornography is something he can manipulate to make himself feel good and possibly alleviate his feelings of loneliness: Every day he knows he can go home, and it will be waiting for him. Mike also likes it; it makes him feel good. All he has to do is open up his device, and there it is. He might feel as if there is so much in his life he cannot control, such as his grades or his friends' opinions about him. Mike may also feel that it is up to him to make himself happy, since no one else is meeting his "needs" for intimacy and safety. Mike might also view the world around him as something to be taken control of—to be used by him for his own ends—because right now, life feels out of control. This mind-set of using the world around him affects how he views other people, especially girls.

4. In light of Christ, how do you think we should see God, ourselves, and others? Explain.

> We might begin to see God is loving and present with us. We might begin to understand that Christ, being God, actually knows our pain and temptations (Hebrews 2:17; 4:15ff). Through Christ, we begin to see that God pursues broken people, and he is committed to changing us and bringing us ultimately into life with him. God is not a cosmic killjoy but is working things for our good and for his glory (Romans 8:28–29). Through Christ, Christians also begin to see others as people to be loved and served, rather

than used (1 John 4:10–11). We also begin to see ourselves as the ones in need of a Savior and as creatures and not the Creator.

THE POINT *(3–5 minutes)*

Summarize, in your own words, one point from this week's lesson.

Give your students time to think, and let multiple students answer.

PRAY

WEEK FOUR:
PORNOGRAPHY

> LESSON GOALS

> LESSON GOALS

1. Explore how pornography interacts with the Tree Metaphor.
2. Explore the concept of pornography through a biblical lens.
3. Explore how knowing Christ informs how we deal with porn.

PRAY

THE SCENARIO

This week, your leader will read the Scenario aloud to you.

> *This week, you (the leader) will read the Scenario aloud to students.* Present the gender-appropriate scenario to your small group.

For Guys:

Brandon is in high school. He loves foreign languages but hates math and science. His grades are suffering in those much-hated subjects. Sitting through those classes feels like sitting through a root canal at the dentist. And no matter how much he works—no matter how much sweat he puts into them—he keeps coming up short, barely scraping by with C's. On top of that, his mom and dad are constantly fighting at home. It seems like every other minute, one of them has ticked off the other. They yell and scream, but nothing ever seems to help them. And the walls of Brandon's room seem paper-thin; he can hear everything . . . constantly.

Brandon also has his own computer and smartphone. About three times a week, Brandon opens up a browser or brings up an app on one of his devices, and he dives in, browsing video after video, picture after picture, of explicit, pornographic material.

Brandon longs for comfort, and he thinks he can find it in the arms of pornography.

For Girls:

Lauren is in high school. She loves foreign languages but hates math and science. Her grades are suffering in those much-hated subjects. Sitting through those classes feels like sitting through a root canal at the dentist. And no matter how much she works, no matter how much sweat she puts into them, she keeps coming up short, barely scraping by with C's. On top of that, her mom and dad are constantly fighting at home. It seems like every other minute, one of them has ticked off the other. They yell and scream, but nothing ever seems to help them. And the walls of Lauren's room seem paper-thin; she can hear everything . . . constantly.

Lauren also has her own computer and smartphone. A couple of times a month, Lauren opens up a browser or brings up an app on one of her devices, and she dives in, browsing video after video, picture after picture, of explicit, pornographic material. Lauren longs for comfort, and she thinks she can find it in the arms of pornography.

SCENARIO REFLECTIVE QUESTIONS *(10 minutes)*

1. In thinking through the Tree Metaphor, what are some soil factors in this person's life? What are some good desires that this person might have? What are some worldviews that might be in play?

> Some soil factors that might be influencing them are their school grades. They cannot necessarily control the subjects where they excel and where they struggle. While they are responsible for trying their best, they just cannot seem to cut it. This adds stress and feelings

Alternate Questions

1. What are some things this person cannot control that are contributing to the situation?

2. What are some things that might make this person want to escape from his or her situation?

3. What are some things this person might want, given all the things in his or her life?

of insecurity to life. Another soil factor would be the war zone of family. They did not choose the families into which they were born. The screaming of parents can add to their own sense of life instability and anxiety. Nowhere, it seems, are they safe from the world around them.

Some desires they might be experiencing are desires for control, refuge, safety, and relief.

Some worldviews that might be in play would be their understanding that God simply cannot, or will not, change their situation. They feel the need to find comfort in porn, rather than God. Perhaps they think porn can offer them what nothing else in their lives can: a refuge from the storm. They might even view porn as simply pictures or movies and not really take into account what exactly is going on in their own hearts and minds every time they choose to engage with it.

2. In what ways can you relate to this person's soil factors?

> This week focuses on the issue of pornography. First, we are going to talk about how to define pornography. Second, we want to talk about how to best follow Christ if we struggle with it.

> **Alternate Questions**
>
> 1. What things in your school or family make you stressed out?
>
> 2. What are some subjects you really struggle in?
>
> 3. How does it feel when your best is not good enough?
>
> 4. What does it feel like when the relationships in your life seem out of control?

THE ISSUE: MATTHEW 5:27–30
(10 minutes)

Ask the following question before reading Matthew 5:27–30:

1. How would you define pornography?

Pornography is any picture, video, story, or other media that we use to sin sexually in thought or deed against God. *You might want to ask your students what they think about this definition.*

Have a student read aloud Matthew 5:27–30.

2. What do you think Jesus is most concerned about in these verses, and how does this relate to the Triad of Life? How do these verses encourage us to think about porn?

Alternate Question

1. What does a lustful heart reveal about a person's thinking about God, self, and others?

> Jesus is most concerned not with content (i.e., pictures, videos, etc.) but with function (the reason why we choose to do certain things). Jesus is most concerned with our hearts and what we are trusting in and turning to, rather than simply external behaviors/factors. This is one of the aspects of the Triad of Life (refer to Week Two for a full description of the Triad of Life): faith. When we define porn, we want to focus mainly on the way in which we use images/videos/thoughts. What matters most is how our hearts engage.

Think back to Week Three: Our hearts are the movers of faith and trust. Porn is ultimately about what we are trusting in for life and salvation. Porn will ultimately lead us to death and judgment. This is where Jesus goes in verses 29–30.

Alternate Question

1. There are other, nonsexual reasons someone might engage with porn. What do you think those would be?

3. What other things, besides lust, do you think would cause someone to want to engage in pornography?

> A person might covet the body image of someone in such a way that his or her desires might be sexualized. Or, like the person in the scenario, someone might choose to look at porn because he or she is desperate for a refuge from life's storms. Some use porn for imitation intimacy. Porn use can feel like a kind of intimacy, but it is really false intimacy because a porn image is not a real person, such as someone the individual knows. Some look at porn to feel more like a man or woman, instilling in themselves a false sense of what men and women actually are. Some use porn out of boredom and even anger that God has not given them actual sexual or romantic relationships.

4. What are some harmful effects of pornography? How might porn affect the way we view ourselves, others, and God? How does porn harm other people?

> Porn never satisfies but instead inflames the lust that is natural to us as sinful people. It twists and distorts people's view of others; they begin to see other people as objects to be used. It dulls their ability to engage in true intimacy with another, especially their future or current spouses.

Alternate Questions

1. Why do you think guys might look at porn? What effects does pornography have on guys?

2. Why do you think girls might look at porn? What effects does pornography have on girls?

3. How do you think porn affects the way we view other people?

4. How might porn affect our view of God?

You can also discuss the differing reasons why girls and guys might look at and be affected by pornography. There are differences here, although there is also a lot of overlap between the two.

For Guys: A guy might look at porn for intense sexual pleasure (facilitating an addictive cycle of seeking more and more pleasure), to feel validated as a man, to covet certain body types in women or men, or as an escape. There are many more reasons as well, and as porn cannot deliver what it promises, pornography usage enslaves the viewer.

For Girls: A girl might look at porn to see what type of body a guy might be most attracted to and how she measures up. She might want to learn about sexual acts and what might be expected in dating. She might covet the body images of other girls, feel validated as a woman, feel intense sexual pleasure, or escape from the world around her.

As we look at porn, we also partner with others in the business of dehumanizing and exploiting the men and women who are performing, many of whom are also enslaved to various drugs to perform the sex acts. Looking at porn also fuels the market for pornography, supporting the companies that produce it and contributing to sexual exploitation and trafficking all around the world.

Pornography also radically affects and damages the way we view ourselves, others, and God. Like the person in the scenario, we might view ourselves as the only ones who can bring relief to our lives. We might be frustrated that we cannot get rid of our sexual urges, so we might see ourselves as the ones who need to take control.

Pornography dehumanizes people and turns them into objects. Ultimately, porn teaches that people exist for our pleasure, a sharp contrast to Jesus's call to love and serve others.

Like the person in the scenario, we might see God as irrelevant to our struggles in life. Maybe we have prayed to him, but he does not answer. Does it ever feel as if God is distant? As if he is just irrelevant? We might even see God as a cosmic killjoy. We might even resent him or be angry with him. How can you relate to these feelings?

Now we are going to take some time to examine pornography in real life. Some of us might never struggle with pornography, but statistically, many of us will. Most likely, you will either struggle or will know someone who does. How do we best follow Jesus in the midst of battling pornography?

THE ISSUE IN LIFE: ROMANS 6:6–14; HEBREWS 12:1–2; HEBREWS 10:24; HEBREWS 3:12–13 *(15–20 minutes)*

Romans 6:6–14

Have multiple students read aloud Romans 6:6–14.

1. What do you think verses 6–7 mean? What hope does this offer to someone caught in the grasp of pornography?

> Believers have been cut off from their old way of life under the dominion of sin by being united to Christ in both his death and resurrection. Our death with Christ severed us from our old way of life. As we were cut off from our old way of life, we were freed from sin's dominion over us, so that we are no longer slaves to it.
>
> While feeling that pornography is enslaving, it does not call the shots for a believer. It is not Lord and Master for believers, no matter how much they might struggle.

2. Given verses 8–11, how does Paul encourage believers to view themselves? Explain.

> Paul encourages believers to view themselves as alive with the same resurrection life that Christ now has, even though that life, for the believer, is a spiritual one (and will be physical one day). Christ's resurrection life is the fountain of our new life in him by the Spirit.

3. In light of the believer's union with Christ, and from verses 12–13, how might someone who struggles with pornography not let sin "reign"? How might he or she not "present" his or her body "to sin as [an instrument] for unrighteousness" and "present" his or her body as an instrument "for righteousness"?

> **Alternate Questions**
> 1. In the moment of temptation, what is one thing a person can do to serve someone else?
> 2. In the moment of temptation, what is one thing a person can do to love God?

> Given their new identity in Jesus, believers can fight pornography with hope. We resist by getting rid of certain access points to pornography, such as a social media account or a smartphone. It will always be helpful to, as a first step, confess the sin to a trusted youth leader or to parents. This certainly includes getting filtering and accountability software, having a trusted mentor have the password for your smartphone, locking down your access to dangerous websites, or even getting rid of technology that poses a problem.

Being "instruments for righteousness" includes living righteously, in accordance with God's ways. When we find ourselves getting bored and being tempted to look at porn, perhaps we can ask, "Could I do the dishes for Mom? Could I go mow the grass? Could I call up a friend for help?" We can also do this through making an intentional plan to read God's Word. We can also look for specific ways to counter the selfishness of porn while loving others in practical ways. Can we think of ways to serve in the youth group? Are there ways to practically serve our family members or our fellow students on a regular basis?

4. What ultimate hope does verse 14 give us and those who wrestle with porn?

> No matter what, believers are not trapped in their sin. God, and his grace through Jesus Christ, is reigning over the believer forever. This means that, through the power of the Spirit, believers can say "no" to porn and "yes" to living a loving, faithful life for Christ. This also means that God will forever grant forgiving and transforming grace.

Hebrews 12:1–2; 10:24; 3:12–13

Have someone read Hebrews 12:1–2; Hebrews 10:24; and Hebrews 3:12–13.

1. What new thing does Hebrews 12:1–2; 10:24; and 3:12–13 add to our discussion? (Hint: Does fighting sin happen only as an individual?) What role does this new thing play in the life of a believer? Explain.

> **Alternate Question**

1. For someone who struggles with porn, what practical ways can you think of for that person to engage more in community with other brothers or sisters?

> Hebrews 12:1–2 introduces the "great cloud of witnesses." The "great cloud of witnesses" is referring to the saints in Hebrews 11, all of whom lived by faith in God and are now cheering on believers toward endurance. One of the reasons the author points this out is that, for our life-race, we will need endurance. We will not always taste or see the goodness of God, but we have to pursue him by faith and trust. Pornography begs us to take our eyes off of Jesus, his kingdom, his plans, and his purposes. But we must, day after day, pray for faith to trust him and to keep living and trusting in his Spirit to work in us. The "great cloud of witnesses" helps us see that we are not alone. Living this life of faith, repentance, and love is possible, but it is possible only in community.

No one can fight sexual sin alone; Hebrews 10:24 and 3:12–13 make this clear. Sexual sin creates a lot of shame and fear in the lives of those who struggle with it. It is necessary, then, for us to live in community with one another. We do not just fight pornography by trying to avoid porn. We fight pornography as other brothers and sisters help us to love others proactively in practical ways, instead of using other people. Others help us to engage in good works, to live out our faith. We can call up someone we trust in the moment of temptation. We can also have accountability partners to whom we can confess and with whom we can pray.

2. Why might "looking to Jesus, the founder and perfecter of our faith" help us in running this race "with endurance"? How can we look to and trust in Jesus today in practical ways?

> When believers look to Jesus, they take their eyes off of themselves and their sin. They focus on Jesus who has triumphed over sin and death, who reigns now in power and authority, and who can help us in our temptation. Not only do we need to run from sin, but we also need to run toward Jesus. We can do this in a number of ways. A good place to start is to cry out to God in prayer when we are tempted. This helps us see that we are dependent upon God and the grace he can give us in Christ. We can also memorize passages of Scripture that remind us of who Jesus is and what he has done for us. It might also mean doing a Bible study or a prayer time once a week with some friends to participate in the community Christ has provided. It certainly means participating in the life of the church. Maybe we can begin to set up a daily time in God's Word (whatever time works best is fine), so that we are filled with the knowledge of Christ and strengthened from his Word. We want to cultivate whatever helps us see Jesus and put our trust in him.

THE POINT *(3–5 minutes)*

Summarize in your own words one point from this week's lesson.

Give your students time to think, and let multiple students answer.

PRAY

WEEK FIVE:
MASTURBATION

> LESSON GOALS:

1. Explore a theology of our sexual desires and masturbation.
2. Explore the Tree Metaphor in relationship to masturbation.
3. Practically explore how Christ helps us to battle masturbation.

PRAY.

THE SCENARIO *(Have a student read this aloud.)*

You are in biology class. The teacher is covering reproductive organs, and for some reason, she makes the off-handed remark, "You know what a great alternative to sex is? Masturbation." The class laughs, and the teacher moves on.

> *The rest of this scenario will be presented by you (the leader). Present the gender-appropriate scenario to your small group.*

For Guys:

Liam just sat there, thinking about the months that had gone by and the almost daily struggle he had been fighting. Normally for him, masturbation is connected to looking at pornography. But it did not start that way, and oftentimes he masturbates when he feels stressed from school. Masturbation has increasingly become a part of his life. What started out as experimenting has turned into a regular habit for Liam, and he wonders, "Is this good for me? Is it really a healthy alternative to sex? Why do I feel guilty? Could I stop if I wanted to?"

For Girls:

As the teacher spoke, Michelle felt as if all the eyes of the class were on her. Recently, she discovered masturbation by exploring herself and her body. She has only done it a few times, and she feels a lot of shame because of it. Before she began to masturbate, she had always heard this was a "guy thing." Now it has become a part of her life, but she does not like to think it is taking over. As she struggles with her shame, she is also shocked by her teacher's words that this is an alternative to sex. She wonders, "Why do I feel so ashamed? Is masturbation really a good alternative to sex? Could I stop if I wanted to?"

SCENARIO REFLECTIVE QUESTIONS *(10 minutes)*

1. If the person in the scenario were raised in a Christian environment, why might he or she feel guilty or ashamed for masturbating?

Alternate Question
1. Do you think this person's guilt could be godly guilt? Why or why not?

For Guys:

If Liam was raised in a Christian context where masturbation was talked about as a sin, how might that contribute to Liam's guilt? Reacting to what he knows his church community would think, perhaps the guilt he feels is more a guilt of letting his family or church community down. Maybe Liam has even come to his own realization that masturbation is not God's best and is, at its core, sinful. Perhaps, then, his guilt comes from an understanding that he has sinned against God.

For Girls:

If Michelle was raised in a Christian context where masturbation was talked about as a sin, how might that contribute to her guilt? Reacting to what she knows her church community would think, perhaps the guilt she feels is more a guilt of letting her family or church community down. Maybe she has even come to her own realization that masturbation is not God's best and is, at its core, sinful. Perhaps, then, her guilt comes from an understanding that she has sinned against God. Her shame might come from feeling as if "girls don't do this sort of thing." She believes that she is somehow other and separate from the rest of the girls, because she struggles with masturbation.

2. Why might the person in the scenario be questioning the goodness of masturbation? What are some things that may or may not be good or healthy about masturbation? Explain.

> *Students can answer this second question in a variety of ways. The main thing is this: Do not shut down the conversation or seek to give simple answers.*

Alternate Questions

1. What else, beyond a physical sensation, is happening when someone masturbates?

2. What happens in the mind?

3. What might be happening spiritually?

People have argued that masturbation can be good because it offers sexual release without actually having sex with someone else. Others see it as a harmless way to reduce stress. Some students know that the Scriptures do not speak directly to this issue, therefore, they believe that it is permissible.

For Guys:

As Liam thinks about this issue, perhaps he has come to the realization that as he masturbates, he is lusting after other people. Maybe he is seeing how focusing on his own sexual "needs" was never God's design for sexuality. Maybe he is realizing that what he perceives as "needs" are simply wants or even idols, i.e., anything we worship and trust in other than God.

For Girls:

As Michelle thinks about this issue, perhaps she has come to a realization that as she masturbates, she is lusting after other people. It might have begun as simply exploring, but now her fantasy life is growing. Maybe she masturbates as a way to relax and comfort herself. Maybe she is seeing how focusing on her own sexual "needs" was never God's design for sexuality in the first place. Maybe she is realizing that what she perceives as "needs" are simply wants or even idols, i.e., anything we worship and trust in other than God.

3. Why do you think the person in the scenario even asks the question, "Could I stop if I wanted to?"

Alternate Questions

1. Why might this person be wanting to stop?

2. What are some things that might prevent someone from simply stopping?

For Guys:

Liam's question helps us see that he might think that stopping would not be possible. Maybe it is the rush and pleasurable feeling that makes stopping it difficult. Maybe it is the pressures of life, and masturbation is a way to feel either in control or simply good in a life that is otherwise stress filled, out of control, or really tough. Masturbation can seem like a good coping mechanism for the stresses or even boredom of life. Getting rid of masturbation might seem like giving up a necessary way to make life tolerable. But the end result of using masturbation for pleasure, comfort, and/or stress relief is incredibly enslaving.

For Girls:

Michelle's question helps us see that she might think that stopping would not be possible. Maybe it is the rush and pleasurable feeling that makes stopping difficult. Maybe it is the pressures of life, and masturbation is a way to feel either in control or simply good in a life that is otherwise stress filled, out of control, or really tough. Masturbation can seem like a good coping mechanism for the stresses or even boredom of life. Getting rid of masturbation might seem like giving up a necessary way to make life tolerable. But the end result of using masturbation for pleasure, comfort, and/or stress relief is incredibly enslaving.

It's helpful to acknowledge that the Bible does not speak about masturbation in particular, but it would be a mistake to think that the

Bible is permissive on the issue. The goal of this lesson is to help students develop a bigger, wider worldview of our Christian lives that leaves no room for masturbation.

THE ISSUE: SONG OF SOLOMON 1:1–4; 3:1–2; 1 CORINTHIANS 6:17–20 *(10 minutes)*

Song of Solomon 1:1–4; 3:1–2

Have a student read aloud Song of Solomon 1:1–4; 3:1–2.

1. What do you think about the sexual desires that the woman in Song of Solomon has? Do you think they are godly or sinful? Explain.

> **Alternate Question**
>
> 1. Do you think God is okay with this woman's sexual passion and drive? Why or why not?

> *Let the awkwardness of the topic and passage sit here for a second. See if your students can come up with their own thoughts regarding their sexual desires.* Ultimately, God gave us our sexuality and desires for pleasure; they are not, in and of themselves, evil. Remember from Week One and Week Two, however, that if they arise from a sinful heart or our flesh, our sexuality will be used in sinful ways. This question helps reveal the truth that God created sexuality.

2. What is the natural state of our sexual desires and our desires for pleasure? Who are they focused on? Explain.

> **Alternate Question**
>
> 1. Do you think your sexual drive and desire for pleasure, now, are as God intended them to be? Explain.

> *The natural state of our sexuality and desire for pleasure is solely concerned with ourselves and what we can gain from sexual experiences. This focuses on the fallenness of our sexuality.

3. Who is the focus of the woman in Song of Solomon 3:1–2? Does she just want the pleasure she can gain from the man? Explain.

> The focus of the women is on her beloved husband. She does not just want the pleasure she can gain from him; she desires intimacy with him. This is a good, God-given desire for intimacy in the context of marriage. This passage reveals what should be the proper focus of our sexuality.

4. How does your answer from question 3 affect how we think about masturbation?

> Masturbation is a self-focused act. Its crowning moment, orgasm, is also the crowning moment of sexual intercourse. Knowing God's design, that moment of orgasm was only meant to be experienced in the covenant of marriage, where each spouse is focused on the other. Masturbation, then, is inherently selfish.

Alternate Question

1. How does the focus of the woman match up with the focus of masturbation? Explain.

1 Corinthians 6:17–20

Have a student read aloud 1 Corinthians 6:17–20.

1. First Corinthians 6:18 says, "Flee from sexual immorality." Paul gives multiple reasons for this in verses 17–20. Starting in verse 17, what do you think they are?

> Starting in verse 17, Paul says that we are "one spirit" with the Lord. This means that, by the Spirit, we are united to Christ. Because of that, Paul tells us to "flee."

In verse 18, if we do sin sexually, Paul tells us that we sin against our "own" bodies, also sinning against Christ, who is joined to us by the Spirit.

In verse 19, Paul tells us that the Holy Spirit, the third person of the Trinity, lives in us. Our union with Jesus, then, includes the Spirit living within us. If we sin sexually, we sin as one in whom the Holy Spirit lives.

Furthermore, at the end of verse 19 and in verse 20, Paul tells us that we have been "bought with a price." The price was the blood of Christ on the cross. Our union with Christ, the fact that the Spirit lives in us, and the fact that we are actually not our own are reasons Paul gives to "flee" sexual immorality.

2. With the information given above, critique the statement, "Who cares if I masturbate or not? It's not harming anyone. I'm my own person!"

> First, because the Christian is united to Christ by the Spirit, when a Christian commits sexual sin, he or she is sinning against his or her own body, which is, in fact, the Lord's as well. Sexual sin grieves not only the Holy Spirit, but it grieves Christ as well because we are united to Him and are his. This feeds into the second part of this statement. Secondly, Christians are not their own. They are not autonomous beings who live in isolation. They have been bought by the blood of Jesus. In that very real sense, Christians belong to Christ, who paid the price for them, purchasing them back from sin and death.

3. When someone chooses to pursue sexual faithfulness, what do you think are some common motivations for giving up masturbation? Compare and contrast these with the motivations Paul gives.

> Some common motivations for stopping masturbation are driven by pride and fear—we do not want to be bad, and/or we fear being punished by God or judged by others. Paul's motivations for pursing holiness are oriented around the person of Christ. They are grounded in who we are in Christ and recall to the Christian's heart the reality that he or she is united to him by the Spirit and share an intimate fellowship with him.

THE ISSUE IN LIFE: HEBREWS 4:15–16; HEBREWS 10:24–25
(15–20 minutes)

Hebrews 4:15–16

Have a student read aloud Hebrews 4:15–16.

1. For students who feel the particular shame of masturbation, what hope can you offer from these verses? What's one way we can "draw near to the throne of grace"?

> Hebrews 4:15 says that Christ is able to understand and empathize with our weaknesses. This means, instead of feeling isolated and ashamed, we understand that Christ has felt our temptations, though he is without sin. We are not other or isolated from him.

> **Alternate Question**
>
> 1. How can Hebrews 4:15–16 dissolve the shame in someone's life?

One particular way we can "draw near to the throne of grace" is to pray. In the moment of temptation or after a moment of failure, we can cry out to God in prayer. Over time, we can learn to pray as our first response to temptation, to rely on Christ and his Spirit to transform us and to provide a way of escape. We can also "draw near" to Christ by reading his Word and even memorizing portions of it.

2. If we are thinking about the Triad of Life, what are some practical steps of faith and repentance a person who is struggling with masturbation can take?

> We can encourage our faith through a number of practices. All Christians need to spend time in the Scriptures—read-

> **Alternate Question**
>
> 1. What are some practical ways we get out of the bathroom or bedroom more quickly than normal to avoid the temptation to masturbate?

ing, studying, and meditating. Through Bible study and reading, we begin to see Christ and our place in the gospel story. We see that Christ is with us, and his Spirit empowers us to grow in holiness. Although tackling the sin of masturbation is difficult, God will be faithful to help us change and will one day make us completely like Jesus, selfless in all respects.

Repentance could mean doing things like actually getting out of the room or house when we are tempted, going to shoot basketball, etc. We could also think through ways to limit our time spent in the bathroom or bedroom.

Hebrews 10:24–25

Have a student read aloud Hebrews 10:24–25.

1. Sexual sin turns us inward, to focus on ourselves. From Hebrews 10:24–25, what practical steps could someone who struggles with masturbation take to foster the aspect of love in the Triad of Life?

> Hebrews 10:24–25 suggests that we should not fight our battles alone. Practically, this could mean phoning a friend and asking for prayer in the moment of temptation. Accountability can be a wonderful gift from God.
>
> It might seem like a stretch, but looking for ways to serve others and use our gifts for the building of God's kingdom is a wonderful way to cultivate selflessness and combat selfishness in our lives. How can we look for ways, in the moment of temptation, to engage in loving service to other people? Perhaps we could do the chores we have been putting off, do an extra load of laundry for Mom and Dad, or unload the dishwasher.

THE POINT (*3–5 minutes*)

Summarize in your own words one point from this week's lesson.

Give your students time to think, and let multiple students answer.

PRAY

WEEK SIX:
HOMOSEXUALITY

> LESSON GOALS

1. Enter into the experience of someone who struggles with same-sex attraction.
2. Explore a theology of homosexuality, including the ideas of gender, and how homosexuality is worked out in the Tree Metaphor.
3. Practically explore the ways in which someone who struggles with same-sex attraction can follow Jesus.

PRAY

THE SCENARIO *(Have a student read this aloud.)*

Remember our story from Week Two? Sarah has always been interested in things that most other girls are not, like working on cars with her dad. She has tried to fit in with other girls, but so far, that is not working.

Throughout middle school, Sarah has also found a home on the soccer team and has continued to play into her first year of high school. Kim, an older girl on the team, has actually taken an interest in Sarah, helping her navigate the high school terrain. Then, a boy in Sarah's class asked her to the homecoming dance. The dance sparked some thoughts within Sarah. She started to realize that she feels attracted to other girls and even now seems to have strong feelings for Kim.

SCENARIO REFLECTIVE QUESTIONS *(10 minutes)*

1. Let's enter into Sarah's experience. How do you think she feels being able to hang out with her dad and having a home on the soccer team?

> Being a part of the family is always a good feeling. Sarah might feel connected in ways that many others might not. Sarah fits in well and feels like she belongs within her family. Sarah feels loved, especially by her father. All of this contributes to Sarah's sense of identity—that she does have a place she can call home. She might also feel, however, that even though she has a home, that home is still not where most girls are. This leads into question two . . .

2. This is a repeat question from Week One, but it is worth thinking about again. For Sarah, how might she be feeling by not fitting in with the other girls because of her attractions? How do you think her gifts play into her feelings?

> Sarah might feel like an outsider, as if she simply does not belong. She might also feel frustrated that she does not belong and wants to grasp onto anything that will make her feel like a normal girl. Sarah is passionate about things like sports and cars, which tend to isolate her from the rest of the girls.

3. If Sarah has never experienced these feelings before, how might she feel knowing that she might be attracted to Kim?

> If she has never experienced these feelings before, Sarah might feel confused. She also might feel excited, as she is experiencing something new. Sarah might also be scared or ashamed, not knowing what this means about her identity and, if she is a Christian, her walk with the Lord. She might wonder if she is gay or bisexual. In other words, this experience could call her whole person into question.

THE ISSUE: EPHESIANS 5:31–32; ROMANS 1:24–27; 28–32; 1 CORINTHIANS 10:13 *(10 minutes)*

Ask the following questions before reading Ephesians 5:31–32.

1. What is our culture's understanding of homosexuality? Why do you think the culture thinks this way?

Alternate Questions

1. How does our culture view our sexual desires?

2. What's the ultimate sexual aim for humanity according to our culture?

> Our culture believes, first, that our desires do not come from *fallen* humans. They come from basically good people. Unless someone is harming another, the culture believes our desires are at worst neutral, and at best, something to be obeyed, followed, and fulfilled at all costs. The culture's understanding of homosexuality flows from this. The concept of orientation is that we are all born with natural orientations that should be followed, because our highest aim is to follow our own selves; our own happiness is the gauge of flourishing humanity. Ultimately, the culture has unmoored itself from the Scriptures as absolute truth and has located absolute truth within each individual. Now each individual has the right to determine his or her own truth.

2. What are your own thoughts regarding homosexuality? Explain.

It is important here to stress the safety of the group, that we are here to walk together toward a better understanding of God, the Scriptures, and ourselves. This is a time for openness and honesty, with the hope that we will refocus ourselves around God and his Word.

Many students will admit that they do not feel that homosexuality is wrong, but that they know that Scripture and the church says it is. It is important to highlight this tension, perhaps asking students to voice how that tension makes them feel, and where they go with it. Other students often can come across as theologically cold, especially when same-sex attraction is just an issue. This is an opportunity to help students both reconcile God's truth with their beliefs and foster compassion for the struggles of same-sex attracted students.

Ephesians 5:31–32

Have a student read aloud Ephesians 5:31–32.

1. Now that we've considered the culture's thoughts and your own thoughts, let's look at God's thoughts. What is human marriage based on? How is the

union that believers share with Christ like the marriage between husband and wife?

> Marriage is based on the relationship between Christ and his church. Among other things, Christ's relationship with the church is intimate—it is concerned with a deep, personal relationship.

> **Alternate Question**
>
> 1. What aspects of Christ's relationship to the church are similar to a husband's relationship with his wife?

2. In light of your answer to question 1, do you think the differing genders are irrelevant or unimportant in marriage? Explain how this relates to the issue of homosexuality and the idea of Christ and his bride, the church.

> Because of this passage (and also Genesis 1:27, Genesis 2:24, and Revelation 19:6–9), gender difference is crucial to marriage and sexuality. The sexual union of a male and female is unique because it brings together two people (who are the image of God individually) to bear the image of God together as one flesh. Same-sex relationships can never achieve the difference that is assumed and crucial to the imaging of Christ's marriage to his bride, the church.

Romans 1:24–27

Have a student read aloud Romans 1:24–27.

1. Going verse by verse, explain this passage in your own words.

2. How does Romans 1:24–27 connect with the Tree Metaphor? From these verses, is homosexual desire and behavior just about what we do with our bodies? Explain.

> It might be helpful here to discuss verse by verse. Verse 24 introduces the

> **Alternate Questions**
>
> 1. What elements of the Tree Metaphor can you see in Romans 1:24–27?
>
> 2. What do you think people who worship creation think about creation?
>
> 3. How do the "dishonoring of their bodies" and the "shameless acts" come about?

categories of lust, heart, and the "dishonoring of their bodies." Lust corresponds to the desires/roots within the tree. The heart corresponds to the seed of the tree. The "dishonoring of their bodies" corresponds to the fruit.

Verse 25 displays how people "exchanged the truth about God for a lie," which corresponds to faulty and sinful worldviews about God—the tree's trunk. Then, people "worshipped and served the creature rather than the Creator." This is clearly fruit, but that behavior is informed by a worldview about creatures. These people have elevated the creature to the level of the Creator and replaced God with created things. People then served created things.

Verse 26 explores "dishonorable passions," which are desires. And finally, verse 27 shows the fruit on the surface, "shameless acts."

Homosexuality, therefore, is not simply about behavior. It is connected to sinful desires and worldviews.

Romans 1:28–32; 1 Corinthians 10:13

Have a student read aloud Romans 1:28–32 and 1 Corinthians 10:13.

1. Can you see yourself in Romans 1:28–32? How? Considering Romans 1:28–32 and 1 Corinthians 10:13, how might these verses change the way you view someone who might struggle with same-sex attraction?

> **Alternate Question**
>
> 1. What do you think these common temptations can be?

> Romans 1:28–32 levels the playing field. It is not just sexual sinners who have replaced the truth about God with a lie to serve idols.

First Corinthians 10:13 says that, despite the uniqueness of someone who struggles with same-sex attraction, there are, beneath the attractions, common temptations that every human faces, including nonsexual desires and worldviews beneath the surface. Common temptations certainly include the temptations to drift away from God's intended purposes and plans and to make oneself a little god.

THE ISSUE IN LIFE: COLOSSIANS 3:1–10; 1 CORINTHIANS 6:9–11; ROMANS 12:4–8 *(15–20 minutes)*

Colossians 3:1–10

Have a student read aloud Colossians 3:1–10.

1. Going verse by verse, what does Colossians 3:1–4 tell us about our identity, and the identity of someone who struggles with same-sex attraction, in Christ? Explain using your own words.

> **Alternate Question**
>
> 1. In light of Colossians 3:1–4, what do you think of the label "gay Christian"?

> Verses 1 and 3 say that those who have trusted in Jesus have been "raised with Christ," which means that we "have died" with him and share in his new, resurrected life. In Paul's words, our life "is hidden with Christ in God." We are not defined by our old ways of life—nor do we live in them anymore—our past slavery to sin, or even our current struggles. We are defined by new, resurrection life in Christ because we are united to him by the Spirit. Paul also says that Christ *is* our life. Our life is not our own; our life is radically defined by Christ and his work in us by the Spirit.

For the person who struggles with same-sex attraction and is a Christian, his or her identity is not a gay Christian; it is simply Christian. There is nothing more basic, encouraging, or even beautiful than being defined simply as a Christ-follower and as a new creation in Christ. According to the Bible, humans are either in Christ or outside of Christ.

2. Because of the Christian's radical, new identity in Jesus, what commands does Paul give in Colossians 3:1–8? If we, ourselves, struggle with same-sex attraction, how can we do these things practically?

> **Alternate Questions**
>
> 1. How can we help someone who struggles with same-sex attraction "seek the things that are above" and "put to death . . . what is earthly" in them?
>
> 2. What are ways we can do these things ourselves, regardless of our struggles?

> Again, it might be helpful to walk verse by verse:
>> Verse 1: "[S]eek the things that are above"
>> Verse 2: "Set your minds on things that are above"
>> Verse 5: "Put to death therefore what is earthly in you"
>> Verse 8: "But now you must put them all away"

Each of these commands can rest under two headings: what to do positively, and what to do negatively. Positively, we are to seek, set our minds on, and concentrate on Christ and his work. Negatively, we are to get rid of, kill, and put away all that is sinful and against Christ.

It's important to help students understand that death brings up the notion of pain and hardship. This life, contrary to the world's understanding, is meant to be lived rejecting our selfishness and even our desire for comfort at all costs. It is also to be lived in radical pursuit of Christ and his plans and purposes.

We can seek Christ by reading and meditating on the Word of God and memorizing it; by finding accountable relationships where sin is confessed and where we pray and encourage one another in Christ; by plugging into a good church where we can practice the sacraments (the sacrament of the Lord's Supper helps us meditate on Jesus) and hear good preaching and teaching. In other words, anything that helps us see Jesus and trust in him is a good thing. We can also prioritize the creation of deep, meaningful friendships with others who can point us to Jesus to counteract the loneliness and isolation that often comes with same-sex attraction.

How can we turn from negative thoughts and behavior? If our same-sex attraction is fueled by looking at pornography, what are some ways we can stop using porn? We can put internet filters and accountability software on phones and computers. If social media and certain relationships are a problem and help to fuel our same-sex attraction, how can we deal with this temptation? We can strategically think through ways to avoid those social media platforms and relationships that are harmful, asking other Christian brothers and sisters to come alongside of us and help us.

1 Corinthians 6:9–11

Have a student read aloud 1 Corinthians 6:9–11.

1. The issue of identity is very important. What do each of these defining characteristics of a Christian mean in verse 11? What does this mean for someone who struggles with same-sex attraction?

> The defining characteristics are "washed," which means we have been cleaned by the blood of Christ; "sanctified," which means that we have been set apart for God by God; "justified," which means we are counted righteous before God (he has counted Christ's righteousness to our account); and "in the name of the Lord Jesus Christ and by the Spirit of our God," which means we belong to Christ and have the Spirit that is now working in us to make us progressively holy.

> As we saw previously, for any Christian who is wrestling with sin, we are defined not by our sin but by who we are in Jesus Christ.

Romans 12:4–8

Have a student read aloud Romans 12:4–8.

1. What aspect of the Triad of Life (faith, repentance, and love) does Romans 12:4–8 talk about? What does this have to do with the same-sex attracted person?

> Romans 12:4–8 builds upon the concept of serving in love. It is important, then, for those who are same-sex-attracted—who may feel isolated, broken, or who may be doubting their worth—to develop and use whatever gifts God has given them for the building up of the body of Christ. If you are helping someone who struggles with same-sex attraction, you should be helping them to discover how their talents and gifts can practically be used in the kingdom of God.

2. Given the Triad of Life, what do you think is the goal of life for someone who is same-sex attracted? Is it heterosexuality? Explain.

> The Triad of Life is faith in Jesus, repentance from sin, and loving God and others. While faith in Christ will gradually change our desires, Jesus never promises heterosexual desires to the same-sex attracted person. He does promise an increasing desire for Jesus and for godliness. While repentance will include fighting same-sex desires, it might not include a transformation to heterosexuality. Repentance, rather, involves turning from sin to Jesus and following him with our faith, desires, worldviews, everyday thoughts, and behaviors. This will result in practically loving and serving others with the God-given gifts and talents a same-sex attracted person might have.

Heterosexuality is not the goal for a same-sex attracted student—holiness is. For someone who struggles with exclusive same-sex attractions, a life of singleness might be the Lord's plan. We need to help students understand that singleness is not a subpar life but can be an extremely meaningful life in intimate relationship with God and others.

THE POINT *(3–5 minutes)*

Summarize in your own words one point from this week's lesson.

Give your students time to think, and let multiple students answer.

PRAY

WEEK SEVEN:
TRANSGENDER

> LESSON GOALS

1. Explore the concepts associated with transgender.
2. Develop a theology of gender.
3. With the concept of the body of Christ, help students think through both how Christ speaks into the lives of those struggling with gender-related issues and how to love and walk beside them.

PRAY

The format of this week is different than the others. Instead of leading the discussion with a personal story in the scenario section, we thought it best to lay out some of the complex issues surrounding the ideas of gender and transgender. There is much confusion today about what is meant by male and female and whether gender is fixed or matters at all for human identity. This lesson focuses on gender identity from a biblical and cultural perspective, and it is important to distinguish these ideas from the medical condition known as intersex. Intersex conditions are disorders of sexual development that occur prenatally and result in difficult decisions regarding the gender of the child. Transgenderism is about the concept of gender as such; intersex conditions are an entirely different category.

THE SCENARIO *(Have a student read this aloud.)*

Currently, there are a host of things associated with transgender. We live in a culture in which many people believe gender is fluid and nonbinary—meaning that "male" and "female" are not the only ways of being human. Transgenderism is a broad term that does not view gender as binary in nature (people being either male or female) but sees gender as a spectrum. The identity label "transgender" is adopted by individuals who reject the traditional view that personal identity is associated with biological sex. Under this category of transgender, there are also individuals who experience gender dysphoria; individuals who may adopt other pronouns not associated with their biological sex; others who see themselves as not having either a "male" or "female" gender based on their biology; those who seek to transition to the other gender using hormones or surgery; and others who, in a broad way, express or experience their gender in ways not aligned with their biological sex.

SCENARIO REFLECTIVE QUESTIONS *(10 minutes)*

1. Explain what these terms mean: biological sex, gender, gender dysphoria, and transgender.

> These terms are important to understand. Biological sex refers to the physical sex someone has at birth, based on their genitalia and their chromosomes. Traditionally, as Christians, we see one's gender as identical to one's birth sex, and there are only two genders: male or female.

There are those who are "intersex," where children are born with ambiguous genitalia due to genetic, anatomical, or hormonal abnormalities. Intersex conditions are distinct from transgender issues in that they are specific medical conditions. These are difficult situations where doctors and parents struggle over what gender an intersex child is. Some argue that intersex conditions are evidence that gender is nonbinary; however, the rarity of the condition suggests that we live in a fallen world, where even our bodies are broken.

In the larger culture, however, gender is taken to mean one's subjective experience of their biological sex, whether one feels it accurately describes their true identity or not.

Transgenderism is a broad term that does not view gender as binary in nature (people being either male or female) but sees gender as a spectrum. The identity label "transgender" is adopted by individuals who reject the traditional view that personal identity is associated with biological sex.

Gender dysphoria is an intense psychological distress that a small number of people experience because of a disconnect between their birth sex and their perceived gender. This intense psychological and spiritual struggle can lead one to take medical, behavioral, and surgical steps to transition to the opposite sex or gender.

2. What do you think gender means?

3. Why do you think God created gender?

THE ISSUE: GENESIS 1:27; 2:18, 20–23; PSALM 139:13–18 *(10 minutes)*

Ask the following questions before reading Genesis 1:27; 2:18, 20–23; and Psalm 139:13–18.

1. One aspect of transgender is the experience of gender dysphoria. Which area of the Tree Metaphor do you think the experience of gender dysphoria most likely falls under? How does this change the way you might think of and approach gender dysphoria or a person who struggles with it?

> Gender dysphoria fits well under the category of the soil of the tree, or contexts we cannot control, though it can also be an aspect of desires (roots), worldviews (trunk), and behavior (fruit). As part of the suffering category, it is an experience, often unchosen, that is the result of the Fall. But the feelings involved in gender dysphoria can also result in any type of behavior, from insisting on being called by different pronouns, to taking opposite-sex hormones, to dressing in ways not aligned with birth sex.

Gender dysphoria is, for many, a consuming and intensely personal struggle, and we should not simplistically see it as a personal, rebellious choice to reject God's binary design. This should really make us approach a gender-dysphoric individual with a compassionate mind-set. Instead of denouncing someone, we need to approach both the issue and the individual with compassion and empathy.

2. Attempt to map out the Tree Metaphor in the contexts, desires, worldviews, and behaviors for someone who expresses or experiences his or her "gender" in ways not aligned with biological sex.

> If we start with the soil, the soil could be the suffering of gender dysphoria. It could also be a context in which gender-norms are pushed hard, such as an overbearing parent or mentor who tries to make a child conform to certain gender stereotypes that are not necessarily biblical. The soil could also be intense trauma, whether physical, emotional, or sexual abuse.

If someone experiences gender confusion, we would certainly expect to find desires for comfort and alleviation from tension and pain. We might find desires to express themselves as the other gender. We might find desires for an affirming community—to have a community to belong to, such as the LGBTQ+ community.

Alternate Questions

1. What contexts could contribute to someone expressing or experiencing his or her "gender" in nonbinary ways?

2. What desires might we find?

3. What trunk/ worldviews about God, ourselves, and others might we find?

4. What fruit might result from this context, these desires, and these worldviews?

In terms of worldviews, we might find anger at God for allowing him or her to be seemingly born in the wrong body. We might find a strong belief that there is no God, because a loving God could not create someone like this. We might even find a strong worldview that says God cannot actually help or alleviate tension because the individual might have prayed, again and again, with no success. A worldview could be that the individual believes he or she is the other gender and he or she must act to express that gender. We also might find worldviews about others that state, "Others must recognize the actual gender that I am"; "others do not understand me or even want to know the real me"; or "others would reject me if they knew the struggle I have within me."

The fruit could be that individuals who struggle with gender dysphoria begin to take an opposite-gender name, dress like the other gender, take hormones of the opposite sex, and/or pursue gender reassignment surgery.

Genesis 1:27; Genesis 2:18, 20–23; Psalm 139:13–18

Have a student read aloud Genesis 1:27; Genesis 2:18, 20–23; and Psalm 139:13–18.

1. What does Genesis 1:27 tell us about being created male or female? How does this change the way we view gender? Explain.

> Genesis 1:27 says gender is created and assigned by God, not chosen subjectively. The meaning of gender is first found in the fact that it is created by God. Second, Genesis 1:27 reveals that both male and female are created in the image of God. They both bear a distinct dignity in their respective genders. Each gender, by itself, images God. This means that one of the reasons God created both male and female is that they, both individually, image him in unique ways. It is important to image God and image God in the gender he gave in his wisdom and love. There is no priority or superiority of either gender.

2. In Genesis 2:18, 20–23, who created gender and why? What difference does this make when we are thinking about issues of gender?

> God created humanity in two genders, and both male and female (Adam and Eve) were called to work together to establish God's purposes for his entire creation—to oversee and manage the entire earth for God's glory. One primary reason for creating two genders is for the purpose of creating children and establishing of family and ultimately human society. Human community flows from the binary nature of gender. The two genders were meant to be interdependent on one another. It makes a difference in that we do not have the authority to define or redefine gender and its meaning in

our lives. Our job is to conform our own thoughts on gender to God's plan and purpose for humanity, not the other way around.

3. What does Psalm 139:13–16 tell us about being created male or female? How might the personal presence and creating role of God, especially verses 17–18, shape our thoughts of gender?

> At first this question and answer might seem trite. But we do want to reframe all of this in light of God's presence. Psalm 139:13–18 says God is intimately involved in the process by which each of us is created. It might be helpful to discuss verse by verse. Verse 13 says God is the one who forms us from birth; he is the one who creates us male or female. Verse 14 says being made by God is a fearful and wonderful thing. God is purposeful when he creates people. Verses 15–16 say no part of the process was hidden from God's eyes; he knew it all.

These verses highlight the truth that God is not only completely in control of how we are formed, but he is also personally involved and present. Verses 17–18 say God thinks thoughts about us, and that those thoughts should be precious to us. This means it matters more what God thinks of us than what we think of ourselves. He has uniquely created each of us.

None of us are freak accidents but rather people whom God cares for intimately. He will guide us to express the gender he gave us in ways that honor him. In other words, God is near and compassionate.

THE ISSUE IN LIFE: LUKE 9:21–24; JOHN 11:25–26; 1 CORINTHIANS 12:14–27 *(15–20 minutes)*

Luke 9:21–24; John 11:25–26

Have a student read aloud Luke 9:21–24 and John 11:25–26.

Alternate Question

1. How is the life of Christ similar to the life of a believer?

1. What does Luke 9:21–23 tell us about Christ and the Christian life in general?

> Because Christians are united with Jesus, we are not only given new, resurrected life in him but we are also conformed to his image through suffering. It might be helpful to walk through verses 21–22. The passage says Christ must suffer and be rejected. Then, Christ will be raised from the dead. This forms the pattern for the believer's life in verses 23–24. The life of Christ is the pattern and power for the believer's life: We are all in this boat of suffering unto glory.

2. What do these verses have to say to Christians who are struggling with their gender and its expression? What might this self-denying, cross-carrying aspect of the Christian life look like practically?

> Verses 21–22 tell the one struggling with gender that Christ has gone through tremendous suffering as well. Christ knows what intense suffering is like. It also tells the student that, though Christ suffered, he was also raised to new, resurrected life, and we will experience the same.

Verse 23 says if we want to follow Jesus, both in suffering and in resurrected life, we must deny ourselves.

Alternate Questions

1. What do verses 21–22 have to do with people who are wrestling with their genders?

2. What do verses 23–24 have to do with people who are wrestling with their genders?

What does that have to do with the student who wrestles with his or her gender? For this person, as for all of us, this must include saying no to our own self-perceptions and temptations to define ourselves. Verse 23 also says if we want to follow Jesus, both in suffering and in resurrected life, we must take up our cross daily. What does this have to do with someone who wrestles with his or her gender? This must mean taking up one's cross by walking daily through suffering and battle; perhaps one way we could all do this better is by making a habit of taking our sufferings to God and laying out our tears and pains before him in prayer.

3. According to Luke 9:24 and John 11:25–26, what is our hope? What difference does that make to our sufferings now?

> The ultimate trajectory and hope of these verses is that we follow Jesus. By following Jesus, we have resurrection life *in* him, and we *have* him. Life *is* Christ, and where Christ is, we will be.

Alternate Question

1. What difference does it make that *life is Christ*, instead of *Christ gives life*?

For the Christian struggling with gender, and for all of us, this makes a difference: True life is found in a person and not a thing or an experience. For those who feel isolated, alone, ashamed, and broken, we have now—and will one day have fully—a person who is both God and man, with whom we will be in perfect relationship forever. We can look forward to the embrace of an individual, who is Christ himself. Christ is not a means to an end (life); He is the end itself.

1 Corinthians 12:14–27

Have a student read aloud 1 Corinthians 12:14–27.

1. What are your general thoughts on this passage?

2. Remembering what we learned from Psalm 139, what does 1 Corinthians 12:14–27 say to individual Christians and to the gender-confused or gender-dysphoric student in particular?

Alternate Questions

1. How might we help a gender-confused or gender-dysphoric person contribute to the body of Christ?

2. How might a gender-dysphoric student better bring God into his or her situation?

> It might be helpful to take these verses in more of a general, overview way, instead of verse by verse. The body is made up of individuals, and each individual has something unique

to contribute to the body. Without one part of the body, the body is incomplete.

How does this speak to the insecurity and alienation a gender-confused or gender-dysphoric student might feel? These students struggling with the gender that God has given have something unique to contribute to the body. We could discover the gifts and talents of that individual and see how those gifts and talents can be used in ways that honor God and build up the body of Christ. We could also help this individual begin cultivating deep and godly relationships with others to counteract the feelings of isolation that gender confusion or gender dysphoria can bring. We could also instill confidence within this student that he or she is safe with us and will not be judged or condemned for the suffering he or she might experience.

It might mean that this person develops intentional times of prayer, Scripture reading, and community where he or she can intimately draw near to the Lord.

3. What does this passage have to do with Christians as a group and those struggling with their gender? How does the fact that you are part of the body of Christ change the way you relate to a Christian struggling with his or her gender?

> Individual Christians are part of a larger organism, the body of Christ. We are all members of one another. It might be helpful to talk specifically about verses

> **Alternate Question**
>
> 1. How might we honor or praise someone who struggles with his or her gender?

26–27. Certainly that means celebrating our unique contributions to the body of Christ, the unique ways in which we contribute to the building up of the church, and not insisting on rigid, nonbiblical gender stereotypes.

It also means that we are to look for ways to encourage such students who wrestle with their gender, looking for ways we can pray for and with them and help them to live out their God-given gender in ways that honor and glorify God.

4. If someone we know comes to us and reveals that he or she is struggling with his or her gender, what might be some helpful responses?

> Perhaps it is better to ask in all circumstances, when someone shares with us a sexual struggle, "Can you tell me more? Can you help me understand your experience?" We can let them know that we are a safe person to talk to, that we will not condemn them or shame them. How might responding in this way help the situation?

THE POINT *(3–5 minutes)*

Summarize in your own words one point from this week's lesson.

Give your students time to think, and let multiple students answer.

PRAY

WEEK EIGHT:
DATING

> LESSON GOALS

1. Provide students with an opportunity to give their own views on dating.
2. Reframe the discussion concerning dating and the question, "How far is too far?" around Christ's two great commandments and what he has done for us.
3. Explore practical ways to date for the glory of God.

PRAY

THE SCENARIO *(Have a student read this aloud.)*

Jonathan is in ninth grade and has just asked out Emily. Jonathan and Emily's friends have boyfriends and girlfriends and are constantly telling them both about everything they're missing. But Jonathan and Emily are thinking differently. They are not simply dating to have a fun experience.

Recently, Jonathan committed his life to Christ and really wants to approach his relationship with Emily in a way that honors Christ. He also wants to honor her and protect both of them from the sexual mistakes he sees his peers making. He is really questioning, "How far is too far? How can we date in a godly way?" Similarly, Emily has been a Christian for years and really wants their relationship to honor God. She is also a little hesitant to date. She wonders, "What's the purpose of dating? What are our intentions?"

SCENARIO REFLECTIVE QUESTIONS *(10 minutes)*

1. In what ways can you relate to Jonathan's or Emily's experience? In what ways is your experience different?

2. How would you answer, "How far is too far?"

THE ISSUE: MATTHEW 22:34–40 *(10 minutes)*

Ask the following question before reading Matthew 22:34–40.

1. What is the world's concept of dating? What do you think the purpose of dating is? Explain.

> The world's concept of dating is essentially self-focused: How can I get what I want from this relationship, and when it is over, how do I break it off cleanly and quickly?

It might be helpful to bring out here that for some students, they will not be allowed to date in high school. Some parents might promote Christian courtship. The point here is that these students will most likely date someone at some time. While many Christians have different ideas on dating, we want to give them general principles to think about dating and being in a relationship with another person that might lead to marriage, both now and in the future.

Have a student read aloud Matthew 22:34–40.

2. How has Jesus fulfilled these two great commandments?

> The obvious answer is that Jesus loved God and loved others. But we want to get students thinking. He loved the Father and doing the Father's will even above his own life. He was willing to suffer the anguish of physical, emotional, and spiritual pain if it meant obeying and trusting in God. Jesus has specifically loved others by dying in his people's place and bearing the wrath of God on their behalf, even though he deserved all worship and praise for who he was (Philippians 2:5–11).

Alternate Questions

1. What does Jesus's prayer in the garden of Gethsemane in Matthew 26:39 reveal about how he viewed God the Father?

2. How has Jesus specifically loved others?

3. How do the Triad of Life (faith, repentance, and love) and Jesus's commandments challenge us to rethink dating and the question, "How far is too far?"

> The world sees consent as a big part of dating. As long as both partners are consenting to sexual acts, those sexual acts are permissible. Scripture, however, teaches that any sexual acts outside of marriage are sinful. Consent only functions in the context of marriage.

> **Alternate Question**
>
> 1. How might the Triad of Life reframe dating?

Christ's words and actions show us that dating is more about considering our relationship with God first. Believers should see their relationship with God as more important than any other person or thing. Christ's words and actions raise new questions: Would God want this relationship for me? How can my relationship glorify God? How can I best serve and love this other person? How can I love this other person as Christ has loved me?

If we live by faith, repentance, and love, then godly dating would include these things. Godly dating would include worshipping and treasuring Jesus more than a significant other, repenting from any type of sexual sin or emotional dependence, and would also include true love, which is sacrificial in nature, putting the other person ahead of our sinful desires.

THE ISSUE IN LIFE: JOHN 15:12–13; 1 TIMOTHY 5:1–2; PROVERBS 7 *(15–20 minutes)*

John 15:12–13; 1 Timothy 5:1–2

Have a student read aloud John 15:12–13 and 1 Timothy 5:1–2.

1. John 15:12–13 points to Christ's sacrifice on behalf of his people. From this passage, what do you think one of the purposes of dating might be? Thinking about the Tree Metaphor, what desires (roots) and worldviews (trunk) would someone have to have if pursuing this purpose in dating?

> One of the purposes of dating is to lay down our lives for each other. This frames the entire discussion around the concept of sacrificial love, rather than using another person for our own sexual pleasure. Focusing on serving each other alleviates peer pressure or thoughts of having the perfect romance. This protects the dating relationship from our own selfish tendencies—our desires for pleasure, comfort, romance, etc. To pursue this selfless way of dating, we must have a desire for the other person to thrive in his or her faith and life. This means wanting the person to grow in his or her relationship with the Lord more than enjoying the dating relationship. It is a very serious matter to lead the person you date into sin.

Regarding worldviews, the person who pursues a sacrificially loving dating relationship sees God as the Lord of the dating relationship. He or she also views the significant other as someone to be loved in sexual purity so that the other person could also follow the Lord. Finally, this person sees himself or herself as contributing to the flourishing of the significant other and not as competing with the other's relationship with the Lord.

2. Given Paul's commands in 1 Timothy 5:1–2, what is a basic way to view each other as fellow Christians? How does this view challenge us in dating? Explain.

Alternate Question

1. How does this family dimension of our relationships challenge how we view dating?

> Paul wants us to view each other as family members: brothers and sisters, fathers and mothers. If we viewed each other as family members first, we would be less willing to enter dating relationships selfishly (i.e., by using another or simply to have fun). We would be concerned with protecting our brother or sister from harm, abuse, or exploitation. We would also be concerned with helping the other thrive in his or her own relationship with God.

3. In light of our discussion so far, what do you think about dating someone who does not believe in Christ?

> *Let the students discuss this and try to steer the conversation in the right direction. This* relationship will end up destroying itself. There will be a Christlike give on one side and only take on the other, with little to no framework for understanding each other. Only one person is actually loving in a Christ-centered, sacrificial way, with God as the ultimate object to be glorified; the other one, even though there may be genuine care and compassion, does not have a worldview where God is the center.

> **Alternate Questions**
>
> 1. What would the relationship look like if one person was loving the other sacrificially and the other was dating in a worldly, selfish way (especially if this other person is not a Christian)?

4. How can we, practically and specifically, respond to Jesus's words and actions from John 15:12–13 while dating? Here is another way to think about this: What are some physical, emotional, and spiritual boundaries we may want to set up in dating?

Leaders, look over this section carefully. Let your students know that you are also someone they can come and talk to if they have questions about their relationships, if they are concerned about where their relationships are headed, or even if they have been abused in a relationship. For further resources, see Appendix A: Thinking through the Issues of Abuse and Rape.

> **Alternate Questions**
>
> 1. What are some ways we can protect ourselves physically while dating?
> 2. What are some ways to protect ourselves emotionally while dating?
> 3. What are some ways to protect ourselves spiritually while dating?
> 4. What are some ways we can guard ourselves sexually while dating?

The principle is to lay down our lives for another person. This means saying no to selfishness and yes to the godly flourishing of another.

Certainly, this brings up physical, emotional, and spiritual boundaries, which often overlap.

Ways to protect ourselves physically are as follows:

We do not watch movies alone anywhere.

Kissing is not an option for us.

We only want to give each other short hugs and not long embraces.

We are not going to hang out or text after a specific time.

Ways to protect ourselves emotionally are as follows:

We do not say, "I love you" until we are moving toward marriage.

We do not use phrases such as "You are the only one for me" or "You are my soulmate."

Ways to protect ourselves spiritually are as follows:

We are not spending extended times of prayer together.

We are not confessing sin to each other, especially of a sexual nature.

You might want a friend, parent, or youth leader who can ask you questions every week about how you are doing in the dating relationship. You might want to ask others to pray for you and your dating relationship.

Proverbs 7

Have a student read aloud Proverbs 7.

1. What imagery is used in Proverbs 7:22–27 to describe the seduced man? How might this imagery apply to dating?

> The first image used is of a dumb ox as it meanders to death. In the same way, we often don't think about the future, or do not think clearly about the present, when dating in risky ways. We often think, "We will only go this far and no further." The problem is, we are already setting ourselves up for failure, by underestimating the danger we are in when we push the limits in dating. The second and third images used show an animal caught in a trap. Oftentimes, relationships can be damaging to us, yet we feel either as if we can't get out, or we don't realize the actual danger we are in. Proverbs 7 wants us to think clearly about the dangers of sexual sin.

2. Can you see yourself in both roles here? In other words, do only women seduce? Are only men seduced? Explain. How should your answer change the way you date?

> Both guys and girls can play each role in this chapter. Guys can be both seduced, and they can seduce. Girls can do the same.

This changes the way we date, because it helps us see that none of us can be trusted; our flesh is at war with the Spirit if we are in Christ. We all need godly boundaries, godly accountability, and a healthy suspicion of ourselves to help us follow Jesus.

3. Translating Proverbs 7:6–9 into our modern context, what are some scenarios that might be similar to "passing along the street near her corner" or "taking the road to her house"? Be specific. At what point in the dating relationship do you think you should identify possible tempting situations for you and the person you are dating? Before or during? Why?

The point is to get your students thinking about dangerous scenarios to be in while dating. Another question would be, what situations can you think of that would be tempting to push sexual boundaries? The following list might help jump start thinking from the group:

> Lingering in cars at night
> Being alone in secluded areas
> Hanging out at parties that do not have parental supervision and/or that will tempt you
> Flirting sexually with someone
> Dressing immodestly

Before getting in a relationship, we should define godly boundaries for ourselves and think through potentially tempting situations in which we could end up in sexual sin. This helps individuals follow Christ from the outset, rather than waiting to see how he or she will react in the moment.

4. In light of our discussion on establishing boundaries, how would you feel doing this in your current (or future) relationship? What are some ways to begin setting up good boundaries to fulfill the two great commandments mentioned above? Explain.

> Having this conversation sets up a plan for the dating relationship instead of doing it on the fly. Setting up good boundaries

begins by first talking about those boundaries, and then enlisting godly people to hold you accountable.

This is best done at the beginning of any relationship, where boundaries haven't already been crossed. We can also invite in a trusted mentor to hold the relationship accountable.

5. Let's say that Jonathan and Emily will not end up getting married. What practical advice would you give them to help their story end well?

6. Thinking about all that we have talked about in the study until now, our new identity in Jesus, and the power that is within us by the Spirit, what are some things you would say to Jonathan and Emily if they had already crossed a sexual boundary? What can we assure them about God? What can we tell them about themselves? What advice might we give them in terms of dating?

> Some things that might be helpful to say to Jonathan and Emily would be:

1. God can, and is willing to, forgive any sin that we commit if we confess to him, repent of the sin, and trust in him (1 John 1:9).
2. We do have the power, now, to live sexually faithful lives because we are new creations in Christ, living in the power of the Spirit (Romans 6:1–14; 2 Corinthians 5:16–17; Colossians 3:1–4)
3. It might be necessary to break off the relationship if neither Jonathan nor Emily can be faithful to Jesus in their relationship.

THE POINT *(3–5 minutes)*

Summarize in your own words one point from this week's lesson.

Give your students time to think, and let multiple students answer.

PRAY

WEEK NINE:
SINGLENESS

> LESSON GOALS

1. Connect the Tree Metaphor to someone who is single, and help students enter into the experience of someone who might be faced with either singleness for a season or singleness for life.
2. Explore a theology of singleness.
3. Explore practical, God-honoring ways to live as a single person.

PRAY

THE SCENARIO *(Have a student read this aloud.)*

Katie's sister, Anna, is getting married. Katie sees how happy her sister is and thinks about how wonderful Anna's life will be now that she has found her husband. Anna is twenty-six, while Katie is only eighteen. But Katie has never dated, and there are no prospects on the horizon. Most of her friends have had multiple boyfriends and girlfriends. Some have even been dating for a couple of years. Finishing up high school and facing the prospect of indefinite singleness, she thinks, "Will I ever meet a guy who likes me?"

Chris, a friend of the family, looks on as Anna takes her vows. Chris has dated a few girls over the years, but as a sophomore in high school, he has already made some dating mistakes. Pornography and messing around sexually have played a big part in his high school career. But he wants to change. He wants to do things differently. But as he looks at the twenty-nine-year-old groom, the goal of staying sexually pure until marriage seems like an insurmountable challenge.

SCENARIO REFLECTIVE QUESTIONS *(10 minutes)*

1. How might Katie feel as she looks in at her sister's wedding?

> Katie might feel as if the reality of marriage is a million miles away, i.e., it will never happen. That might bring up feelings of loneliness, frustration, panic, anxiety, and despair. It might be helpful to tease out each of these feelings with your students: why might she despair? Why might she panic?

2. For Chris, why might "staying sexually pure until marriage" seem "like an insurmountable challenge"? Can you relate to Chris? Why or why not?

> Chris has already engaged in sexual sin, and he might not see an end in sight. He might also have tried to simply stop a lot of his behavior but has had little success. He might have prayed to God but does not feel as if God has actually done anything.

3. What are your views on singleness? What are some unique challenges that someone who is single either for an extended time in life or for all of life might face?

> Some see singleness as a fun, free future. Others might see singleness as something to dread and are panicked at the thought. In terms of unique challenges, singles face the prospect of never having the sexual, physical, and emotional intimacy of marriage. Singles also face the challenge of fostering intimacy with other people without having sex. Single people might also have to face the challenge of many painful breakups. They might also face the challenge of never having a new biological family to be a part of.

THE ISSUE: 1 CORINTHIANS 7:29–35 *(10 minutes)*

Before reading 1 Corinthians 7:29–35, discuss the first two questions.

1. Imagine a single person, either single for life or for a season. Describe the different possible aspects of their Tree Metaphor (soil, roots, trunk, fruit).

> Possible soils could include being in school and dealing with the prospect of not being married anytime soon; being immersed in

the hook-up culture during college; pressure from church people to get married and have kids; not feeling like you are attractive or desirable as a dateable or marriage-able man or woman; or not being in a church context that takes care of its single members and connects them in good relationships with others.

Possible roots/desires could be to please the Lord and walk faithfully with him; desires to avoid being a despairing single person but to contribute to community and the church; desires for companionship and to belong, to feel a part of a loving relationship or even to be married; desires to branch out into sexual promiscuity despite knowing that sex is reserved for marriage; desires to live selfishly, regardless of the consequences.

Possible trunks/worldviews about God could include: He is here with me; he seems absent and uncaring. People's worldviews about themselves could include: *I absolutely need to have a boyfriend/girlfriend or husband/wife to have a fulfilled life. I am going to use singleness to serve other people to the best of my ability. I am not complete without someone else. I must take matters into my own hands. I am fulfilled in a relationship with Christ and can trust him to give me what I need.*

Possible sinful fruit/action could include participating in the hook-up culture; serial dating with the mind-set that this will make life meaningful, hoping that the next relationship will be fulfilling; idolizing a current relationship. Possible godly fruit/action may include godly contentment and involvement in the local church; making lots of friends and developing community and intimacy.

2. What are some assumptions about single people that our culture or other Christians might have? What do you think about these assumptions? Explain.

> Some assumptions the culture might have are that being single and sexually active is the freest and best life. In the culture's eyes, to be single and without a sexual outlet might be seen as the worst, most tragic form of life. Some people might assume that there is something wrong (physically, emotionally, mentally, etc.) with single people, that they might be socially awkward or have an

annoying personality. Christians might pity single people, thinking that they are missing out on the wonderful, "life-making" benefits of marriage or simply pining away in loneliness.

Have a student read aloud 1 Corinthians 7:29–35.

3. In 1 Corinthians 7:29–35, how does Paul describe the single person and that person's life? How does Paul's understanding of the unmarried Christian life match up or differ from cultural stereotypes of singleness?

> **Alternate Question**
>
> 1. What does it mean to "not be divided" when you are single?

> Paul's understanding of the unmarried Christian life clashes with both the cultural and Christian stereotypes of singleness. It might be helpful to go verse by verse here. First, Paul warns the Corinthians that Jesus is coming back soon. Even though Paul wrote this in the first century, we are still to be on guard for Christ's return. He motivates people with that truth and encourages them to live in that reality. Paul wants those to whom he is writing to be free from anxiety, but notice how each person, single or married, has various anxieties that must be addressed. The single person is, for Paul, able to be concerned about and devoted to the things of the Lord. Paul also describes the single person's life as one that is "not divided."

In contrast to cultural stereotypes about singleness, Paul does not view the single and sexually active lifestyle as the most life-giving. He sees the unmarried single life most fulfilled in devotion to worship of the Lord and ministry to other people in rich relationships. Paul's view of the unmarried Christian's life is one that is outward focused, serving others, not inward-focused, serving the self.

In contrast to Christian stereotypes about singleness, Paul does not see marriage as the better life. Instead, Paul thinks singles have the best lives. The single person has undivided interests. It is not godly or biblical to devalue the single life; we should treasure it.

4. What are some expectations about singleness that you might have that Paul would not have?

5. Given Paul's words, how might single people, even as students, practically devote themselves in an undivided way to the Lord? How do we fight against the pressure to be always in a dating relationship? Explain.

> Part of this is identifying people's gifts and how they might be used for the building up of others and for the worship of God. We could look out for younger brothers and sisters in Christ to encourage, pray with, and mentor. We could devote ourselves to evangelism in our schools, in developing gifts and talents, in thinking about ways to get involved in the youth group, etc.

> **Alternate Question**
>
> 1. What are some practical ways you can focus on loving God and loving people in this season of life?

Ultimately, we want to communicate that singleness is about ministry to others.

6. Does question 3 change your view of the single life? Why or why not?

This is a question for all those who are not buying into Paul's vision of the single life. This is a chance to expose the worldviews, desires, and identity battles that we all face.

> **Alternate Question**
>
> 1. What desires and worldviews feed into your answer to question 4?

Depending on the answers given by students, you will want to uncover the worldviews and desires behind their answers. Consult Question 1 in the first section of the Issue for a list of these.

THE ISSUE IN LIFE: 1 THESSALONIANS 5:14; ROMANS 8:28–39 (15–20 minutes)

1. Let's think through the Triad of Life (faith, repentance, and love) and singleness. What does faith look like for the unmarried Christian? What are some specific things an unmarried Christian might have to repent of? How can an unmarried Christian love others and love God in specific ways?

> Part of this involves examining the ways we can love others intimately, even though we might not be married. Intimacy might mean finding close friends to meet with regularly, finding a way to get involved in a ministry at a church, or finding ways to mentor others, etc. It could be boiled down to find ways to "know others" and "be known by others" in real and honest ways.

Alternate Questions

1. How can we love others intimately, even though we are not married?

2. What do you think intimacy is? How does that play out in the unmarried Christian's life?

1 Thessalonians 5:14

Have a student read aloud 1 Thessalonians 5:14.

1. What does each verb (admonish, encourage, and help) in 1 Thessalonians 5:14 mean? In carrying out 1 Thessalonians 5:14, how might an unmarried high school student practice Christian community? Be specific.

Alternate Questions

1. What might be some things we, as single people, need to be warned of, or instructed about?

2. What might be some things we, as single people, need to comforted and consoled about?

3. Why would we, as single people, need someone to commit to looking out for us?

> Even though you take each verb in turn, help the group to notice that each verb means that we actually need people to speak into our lives about these matters. This brings up the idea of mentorship, accountability, and community.

To admonish means to warn or instruct. We need to be warned about the possible sin in our lives and friend groups.

To encourage means to comfort and console. We need comfort and consolation when we sin, and to be reminded that we are forgiven in Christ and that he, by his Spirit, is working in us. When there is suffering in life—when we are worried about finding a spouse, when we have had a bad breakup, or when we are simply feeling weary, alone, and isolated—we also need comfort and consolation.

To help means to be devoted to or to care for another. Paul gives this command to Christians so that they will be committed to each other. The principle is that we cannot do life on our own. We need trusted friends, youth ministers, mentors, pastors, family, and others to meet with us, pray with us, and really know us.

Romans 8:28–39

Have a student read aloud Romans 8:28–39.

1. What things might be hard to believe about Romans 8:28–39 given this discussion on singleness? How does Romans 8:28–39 speak both to Katie, who wonders if she will ever find the right guy, and to Chris, who wonders how he will stay sexually pure until marriage? How does Romans 8:28–39 speak into your situation?

These verses can sometimes be used as a Band-Aid and a quick fix. We need to wrestle with them and our experience. Let your students express the tension.

> It might be helpful to discuss verse by verse. Katie, Chris, and we need to know that life is not random, and it is not up to chance. God has planned each step of the way for us, and his purposes for us are certain and cannot be changed. God is orchestrating all things for our good and his glory (vv. 28–29).

God is committed to making us like Jesus and bringing his work in each of us to completion (vv. 29–30). Katie needs to know that God is working at all times, and that he

Alternate Questions

1. How does knowing that no charge can be brought against God's people because of their sin change the way we live as sexually struggling, unmarried Christians?

2. As an unmarried Christian, what difference does knowing that Jesus prays for you make in your life?

3. How does the prospect of being with Jesus change the way we live now as unmarried Christians? How does the fact that Jesus is with us now, by his Spirit, change the way we live now as unmarried Christians?

is working for her good in her singleness. Chris needs to know that God will continue his work in Chris to conform his character to Christ even in the midst of sexual temptation.

Chris also needs to know that his sin does not outmatch the righteousness of Christ given to him (vv. 31–34). Jesus has paid for him, and no charge of sin can change that.

Another wonderful truth about this passage is that Jesus *himself* is interceding for us (v. 34). He is constantly bringing our troubles and sufferings before the throne of the Father. In other words, we are not alone in our prayers. Jesus, the Son of God, prays for us.

It is also a strengthening and motivating truth to know that God is with us and for us. If we are wondering if we will ever find "the one," we know that whatever happens, God has not left us or abandoned us. God will give us what we really need and ultimately really long for, and that is Jesus himself (vv. 35–39).

THE POINT *(3–5 minutes)*

Summarize in your own words one point from this week's lesson.

Give your students time to think, and let multiple students answer.

PRAY

WEEK TEN: MARRIAGE

> LESSON GOALS

1. Explore how marriage points to Christ and his church.
2. Explore how Christian marriage is a ministry to others, just like Christian singleness and the Christian life in general.
3. Explore the relationship between Christ and his church and how that spurs us on to live the Triad of Life.

PRAY

THE SCENARIO *(Have a student read this aloud.)*

Christina and Matt are getting married. As they near the end of the service, their minister turns to Matt: "Will you, Matt, have this woman to be your wedded wife, to live with her after God's commandments in the holy state of marriage? And will you love her, honor and cherish her, so long as you both shall live?"

Matt responds, "I do," and then repeats after the minister: "I take you, Christina, to be my wedded wife, and I do promise and covenant, before God and these witnesses, to be your loving and faithful husband, in plenty and in want, in joy and in sorrow, in sickness and in health, as long as we both shall live."

SCENARIO REFLECTIVE QUESTIONS *(10 minutes)*

1. What are your first impressions of the vows written above? What stands out to you? Is there anything you think is really good about them? Does anything seem weird?

2. What worldviews about God, others, and self would someone need to keep their commitment to the vows listed above?

> God keeps his covenant promise with us, and he empowers us to keep covenant as well. God is also a God to be followed at all costs. His Lordship is supreme, not my happiness.

There are going to be times when loving my spouse will not be easy and when I will not be easy to love. The covenant means that my spouse, regardless of how I feel in the moment, is someone to be loved and served.

There is joy in keeping covenant with my spouse and true life is not found in living for myself. I am meant to be totally committed to my spouse. This is not a 50/50 contract.

3. Compare and contrast these vows with what you think most people in the culture think about marriage.

> Unlike the culture, which has a selfish and temporary understanding of marriage—a 50/50, you-do-your-part-and-I'll-do-mine agreement—these marriage vows are covenantal, requiring one hundred percent commitment from both spouses. For the culture, marriage is just two people. But for the Christian, the covenant is between husband, wife, and God in the sight of the church. Culture views marriage as nonpermanent and ultimately not necessary, given the mindset of hooking up and cohabitating. Christians see the covenant of marriage as permanent except in cases such as adultery, abuse, neglect, and abandonment.

> **Alternate Question**
>
> 1. For the culture, who are the parties involved in the marriage ceremony? What difference does this make to how one views marriage?

THE ISSUE: EPHESIANS 5:22–33; MATTHEW 22:30; REVELATION 19:6–9 *(10 minutes)*

Ephesians 5:22–33

Have a student read aloud Ephesians 5:22–33.

1. What bigger story is human marriage supposed to tell? What specific details or aspects of this story is marriage supposed to display?

> The bigger story of human marriage is that of Christ and his church. The relationship between husband and wife is supposed to put on display certain, specific characteristics of the relationship between Christ and his church. You might want to go verse by verse here.

In verse 22, wives are called to submission. Wives are supposed to submit to their husbands in a manner similar to the way the church submits to Christ by trusting his character and leadership. There are a couple of things to note. The church is valuable and loved by Christ; her value is shown by Christ giving up his life for her. The church is to trust Jesus because of who he is and what he has done for her. The church is also not submitting to a selfish and domineering tyrant. She is submitting to Christ, who is selfless, loving, and serving. Within a marriage, submission does not mean allowing physical, sexual, or emotional abuse to take place.

In verse 25, human marriage is meant to demonstrate the sacrificial love of Christ for his church, and this applies directly to husbands. Husbands are to love their wives in a sacrificial way, as Christ loves the church, leading them by service and love, rather than by domination and oppression. In verses 26–27, husbands are to love their wives, helping them grow to be more like Christ in godliness and holiness.

This brings into view holiness, which is one of the goals of marriage. Christ loves his church and will present her to the Father in perfection, beauty, and godliness. In a similar way, marriage is meant to be for the purpose of each spouse's growth in godliness.

In verses 28–33, marriage is meant to model the oneness and unity Christ shares with his church. Man and woman are one flesh, even though they each remain individuals. They share one life and a common goal as if they shared one body.

Marriage is a ministry of love and submission, leading to holiness.

Matthew 22:30

Have a student read aloud Matthew 22:30.

1. What is the resurrection? How does that relate to marriage?

Alternate Questions
1. What happens at the resurrection?
2. What happens to marriage at the resurrection?

> The bodies of both believers and unbelievers will be raised to imperishable life: believers will be raised to life and communion with God, and unbelievers will be raised to continual punishment and separation from God.
Human marriage is done away with at the resurrection.

2. How might our Christian culture be shocked by Matthew 22:30? Explain.

> Christians sometimes tend to think that marriage is the be-all-to-end-all. We might be shocked to know that human marriage is only temporary, not eternal.

Revelation 19:6–9

Have a student read aloud Revelation 19:6–9.

1. In light of Revelation 19:6–9 and Matthew 22:30, will there be marriage in heaven?

> Yes, there will be marriage in heaven, although that marriage will not be between individual humans. There will be a marriage between Christ and his bride, the church.

2. In verse 9, what does the Lamb have to do with the prophecy of Genesis 3:15 mentioned in Week Two, "I will put enmity between you and the woman, and between your offspring and her offspring; he shall bruise your head, and you shall bruise his heel"?

> We talked about this in Week Two. This question is to help students connect the dots from the beginning of the Bible to the end. Ultimately, the prophesied offspring of Eve was bruised by the serpent in his suffering and death on the cross as the sacrificial

Lamb of God. Christ was sacrificed in our place, for our sins. And yet, it was actually through his sacrifice as the Lamb of God that he crushed the head of the serpent, meaning he defeated sin, death, and all the powers of evil.

3. How did the Lamb love his bride? What does this have to do with Ephesians 5:25? How might this vision work out practically for husbands?

> One of the most crucial aspects of marriage is sacrificial love. The Lamb loved his bride by dying in her place, by bearing the wrath of God so that she might be forgiven, cleansed, and made holy. This is what Ephesians 5:25 means when Paul says that Christ "gave himself up for" his bride.

For husbands, this means that their vision for loving their wives must include sacrifice: not death on a cross, but death to selfishness and sin. Practically, this means doing the dishes (service and help around the house), taking care of the kids, saying no to selfish ambition in terms of a job that might ruin a family, or saying no to selfish amusements and entertainment that might neglect or hurt a wife and family. Husbands are to say no to being passive (think: sitting on the couch and being absorbed in the TV) and yes to being engaged in the family (think: playing with kids, truly taking the time to ask good questions of a wife and be there for her, taking the time to pray with the family, etc.).

4. How does the "fine linen, bright and pure" and the "righteous deeds of the saints" in Revelation 19:8–9 relate to Ephesians 5:26–27? How does this shape your view of marriage?

> Christ's work in Ephesians 5:26–27 produces the "fine linen, bright and pure" and "righteous deeds" of Revelation 19:8–9. Marriage should produce godliness and holiness. Marriage is not simply for personal, earthly happiness but for our eternal joy and godliness.

Marriage is not a self-absorbed work about a couple's personal needs. Marriage is a ministry, even a calling, meant to help each other follow Christ and walk in holiness.

THE ISSUE IN LIFE: PHILIPPIANS 2:1–13 *(15–20 minutes)*

Have a student read aloud Philippians 2:1–13.

1. What is the relationship between verses 1–5 and verses 6–11? Explain the verses and sections.

> Verses 1–5 say what we should do. Verses 6–11 say why we should do it and to whom we should look for the power to do it.

Alternate Questions
1. What does verse 1 tell us?
2. What does verse 2 tell us?
3. What do verses 3–4 tell us?

Verse 1 says that there is encouragement in Christ, comfort from love, participation in the Spirit, affection and sympathy between believers. There is a real unity here.

Verse 2 says to be "of the same mind." This means that we are to be on the same page with how we act. In other words, our actions toward each other come from the fact that we are all part of the same body, that we all have a vested interest in treating each other in the same way.

This section urges us to put away selfishness and pride, to take on a humble mind, thoughtfully doing what is best for others.

Verses 6–11 tell us why we should do verses 1–4 and whom to look to for the power to do it. Verses 6–11 recap the story of Jesus's faithful obedience to the Father in leaving his glory and power to serve and die on the cross for the church. The Father rewards his Son's faith and obedience to his will by resurrecting him from death and seating him at his right hand. This resurrected and glorified Jesus is enabling us to live as he did, looking after the interests of others.

2. Practically, how might we do verses 1–4 in our families? How might we do verses 1–4 at school?

> As students, we might help Mom out with chores without asking. We might ask our moms and dads if there is anything extra we could do to help out the family. We could intentionally spend

time with younger siblings, playing with them or even doing special things for them. We could spend time intentionally praying for our families.

As students, we might keep an eye out for the kid who does not have many friends. We might sit with him or her in the lunchroom or invite him or her to hang out after school or come to youth group. We might voluntarily take up others' lunch trays to the trash. We might defend a student who is being bullied. We might start a Christian club to reach out to our classmates. We might volunteer our time to help tutor another student.

3. How does the normal Christian life of Philippians 2:1–11 relate to the married Christian life of Ephesians 5:22–33? How does this shape our understanding of marriage?

> **Alternate Question**
> 1. What must you do to have an ultimately good and godly marriage?

> They match up! Except for the specific roles of husband and wife (submission, leadership, and marital love), the general character of marriage, that of a sacrificial relationship with someone else, matches up to how we should be as Christians with one another.

This should change our view of marriage in a couple of ways. Romantic emotions in marriage are great, but so much of marriage is about living the normal Christian life in seeking the others' best. Our understanding of marriage flows from our general understanding of the Christian life. We can have a fulfilled Christian life without ever being married, but marriage is also an extension of the life we should already be living as a Christian. You must be living the Christian life! If we are not, our marriages will suffer and break down.

4. What does Philippians 2:1–11 indirectly say about faith and repentance?

> **Alternate Question**
> 1. Whom are we to be trusting in while trying to live out Philippians 2:1–4?

> Philippians 2:1–11 is directly about the love aspect of the Triad of Life, but it speaks to and depends on faith and repentance as well. We are to look to Jesus for the motivation and the power to do what he

commands. Paul also assumes that we are repenting from our self-ish way of life to live in service toward one another.

5. How does the concept of working out our salvation (Philippians 2:12–13) relate to the holiness Christ produces in his church (Ephesians 5:26–27; Revelation 19:8–9)? Relate this to living sexually faithful lives, in light of our union with Christ.

> **Alternate Questions**

> 1. What does Philippians 2:12–13 mean for marriage?
>
> 2. What does Philippians 2:12–13 mean for our sexuality?

> In Ephesians 5:26–27, Christ works to produce holiness in his church, and that church is clothed with that holiness in Revelation 19:8–9. While Christ produces the holiness, the good deeds are still said to be hers. Philippians 2:12 says that the church is involved in producing her holiness and good works. She is not passive but engaged and working hard. Even so, as the church works, she is to do so because God is working in her "to will and to work for his good pleasure" (Philippians 2:13).

Marriage will be hard work and will involve our effort and perseverance in trusting in Christ and in loving others. We must also understand that Christ is working within marriages; it is not all up to us.

This also means that God requires me to work hard for sexual holiness while understanding that he is working as well in us by his Spirit. We can say with Paul that, because God is working in us, "he who began a good work in you will bring it to completion at the day of Jesus Christ" (Philippians 1:6).

THE POINT *(3–5 minutes)*

Summarize in your own words one point from this week's lesson.

Give your students time to think, and let multiple students answer.

PRAY

APPENDIX A:
THINKING THROUGH THE ISSUES
OF ABUSE AND RAPE

This workbook does not directly address the topics of sexual abuse or rape, but within the course of a discussion on sexuality, a student may disclose being the victim of these sexual crimes. While the curriculum will not ask students if they have been abused, we hope that the supportive environment of your small group will give them permission to talk about anything they want, including experiencing abuse or rape.

As a leader, responding with kindness, grace, and skill is of utmost importance for students who choose to disclose sexual abuse that they have endured. Many small group leaders may feel inadequate and untrained to handle these situations, and that is okay. Know that responding well to an abuse disclosure means you should reach out for help. We have included trusted resources that can be contacted during an emergency. We have also included a starting point for a biblical response.

A STARTING POINT

In the moment, if students disclose sexual activity that was forced upon them—either physically or through manipulation—remain calm and allow the students to reveal as much or as little as they are able. Do not ask leading questions, but if you feel it is appropriate, ask open questions such as, "Is there anything else you would like to tell me?" Be calm and open to whatever students may tell you. Believe the students. The likelihood of a child or teen lying about abuse or rape is very low. Affirm biblical truths for the students, such as, "This was not your fault; you are not to blame; I will help you."

If students are in danger, act immediately; and, if you are a small group leader, contact your youth minister. Call the authorities and do not allow students to return to any environment where they might be abused again.

When the students have left your immediate care, know that your responsibilities may not be finished yet. First and foremost, remember that rape and sexual abuse are crimes. Your state may require you to report the abuse to the authorities. Check to see if you are a mandated reporter (this should be done before the small group begins). If you are a mandated reporter, follow your state's procedure for reporting disclosures of child abuse. However, even if you are not legally required to report, report anyway. Sexual abuse and rape need to be prosecuted. It is in the best interest of the child and the community for the authorities to be notified about these crimes.

Students will likely need care from a counselor trained in trauma therapy. Anyone who has survived sexual abuse or rape has endured a deep evil. It would be wise for church leaders to compile a list of local counselors who are experienced in helping teens heal from childhood trauma.

RESOURCES FOR THINKING ABOUT SEXUAL ABUSE

RECOMMENDED ORGANIZATIONS

GRACE (Godly Response to Abuse in the Christian Environment) — www.netgrace.org

Darkness to Light — www.D2L.org

Church Protect — www.churchprotect.org

Diane Langberg and Associates — www.dianelangberg.com

Together We Heal — www.together-we-heal.org

EDUCATION, PREVENTION, AND RESPONSE

The Child Safeguarding Policy Guide for Churches and Ministry, by Basyle Tchividjian and Shira Berkovitz (New Growth Press, 2017)

Protecting Children from Abuse in the Church, by Basyle Tchividjian (New Growth Press, 2017)

Caring for Survivors of Sexual Abuse, by Basyle Tchividjian and Justin Holcomb (New Growth Press, 2017)

What the Bible Says to Abuse Survivors and Those Who Hurt Them, by Victor Vieth (New Growth Press, 2017)

The Spiritual Impact of Sexual Abuse, by Diane Langberg (New Growth Press, 2017)

"Faithful Protection," by Beth Hart and Mike Sloan (available for download at www.faithfulprotection.org)

"What Is Child Abuse and Neglect? Recognizing the Signs and Symptoms" (available for download: https://www.childwelfare.gov/pubPDFs/whatiscan.pdf)

On the Threshold of Hope: Opening the Door to Hope for Survivors of Sexual Abuse, by Diane Langberg (Tyndale House, 1999)

GLOSSARY

Biological sex: People's God-given gender, either male or female, corresponding to their physical anatomy. God-given gender and biological sex are identical. *Scripture References: Genesis 1:27; Psalm 139:14.*

God's covenant of grace: In God's covenant of grace, God "freely offereth unto sinners and salvation by Jesus Christ; requiring of them faith in him, that they may be saved, and promising to give unto all those that are ordained unto eternal life his Holy Spirit, to make them willing, and able to believe."[1] *Scripture References: Genesis 3:15; John 3:16; Romans 10:9.*

Context: Part of Harvest USA's Tree Metaphor, corresponding to the soil of a tree. The context includes everything we cannot control in life. Because of the fall and the broken world we live in, our natural context includes our sufferings, and the new context of a Christian includes the church. *Scripture References: Genesis 3:16–19; 1 Corinthians 12:18–20.*

Community: The Christian's vital relationship to others, particularly the body of Christ (the church), where believers are practicing love toward others, confession of sin, and encouragement of one another. *Scripture References: Matthew 22:37–40; Galatians 6:1–2; Hebrews 10:24; James 5:16.*

Desire: A longing for something or someone. Desires are either of the flesh or of the Spirit, either sinful or righteous. Because of the presence of the Spirit and the flesh within the believer, the experience of desire can oftentimes be mixed. *Scripture References: Galatians 5:16–23; James 1:14–15.*

Faith: General faith consists in knowledge of, agreement with, and trust in something or someone. Saving faith consists in knowledge of, agreement with, and trust in Jesus Christ as Savior and Lord. Faith is one aspects of the Triad of Life (faith, repentance, and love) that forms the basis of the Christian life. *Scripture References: Scripture References: Mark 1:14–15; Hebrews 11:1; John 20:31.*

---

1. *The Westminster Confession of Faith with Scripture Proofs in the English Standard Version* (Lawrenceville, GA: Presbyterian Church in America Christian Education and Publications, 2013), 26.

The Fall: The event where Adam and Eve, who represented the human race, rejected God and spiritually killed and enslaved mankind to sin. As a result, every human is born guilty of sin, is corrupted totally by it, and actually sins all the time in relation to God. *Scripture References: Genesis 3:1–18; Romans 3:10–23; 5:12; Ephesians 2:1–3.*

Flesh: The totalizing, corrupt nature of the unbeliever that rebels against God continually. In the believer, the flesh is not the totalizing nature but is present nonetheless and wars against the Spirit. *Scripture References: Romans 8:3–7; Galatians 5:16–23.*

Fruit: Part of Harvest USA's Tree Metaphor, corresponding to our behaviors. Fruit is a product of a host of worldviews, desires, and the context in which we find ourselves. Fruit can either be evil or good. *Scripture Reference: Luke 6:43–45.*

Gender dysphoria: The experience of an individual who feels as if his or her birth sex does not match up to his or her actual identity.

Gender: The secular culture sees gender as based in feeling and experience, whereas Christians see gender and biological sex as the same. Our gender, then, is not an experience or feeling we have but an objective reality given to us by God. *Scripture References: Genesis 1:27; Psalm 139:14.*

Guilt: Personal guilt is being accountable to punishment, because of who we are (sinners) and what we do (sin). *Scripture References: Leviticus 5:14–19; Isaiah 6:7; Luke 23:22.*

Holiness: The quality of being holy, and to be holy is to be set apart from sin by God and for God. The believer is both holy and is called to pursue holiness in godly living. *Scripture References: 1 Corinthians 6:11; Colossians 1:13; Hebrews 12:4; 1 Peter 2:9.*

Human heart: The human heart is the mover of faith and trust, defines us as individuals, and is what the Lord is most concerned with in our lives. It can even be thought of as our nature. The human heart is either fallen and corrupt or alive and made new. *Scripture References: Genesis 8:21; Deuteronomy 6:5; Jeremiah 17:9; Ezekiel 36:26; Romans 10:10.*

Intersex: The condition of someone who is born with ambiguous genitalia, i.e., reproductive organs that have characteristics of both male and female.

Love: Sacrificial action on behalf of another. *Scripture References: John 15:12–13; 1 John 4:10–11.*

Lust: An overmastering desire for something contrary to God, oftentimes sexual in nature. *Scripture References: 1 Thessalonians 4:5; Titus 3:3; 2 Peter 2:10.*

Marriage: A covenant relationship between one man and one woman for life, in the eyes of God and the church, pointing to Christ's relationship with his church. *Scripture References: Genesis 2:24; Ephesians 5:22–33.*

Masturbation: Sexual self-stimulation.

New man: The new self of a Christian is filled with the Spirit, free from slavery to sin, and lives now in the power of Christ. In Christ, believers have been re-created after the image of God in true knowledge, righteousness, and holiness. *Scripture References: Ephesians 4:22–24; Colossians 3:9–10.*

Old man: The fallen, natural, corrupt self that is filled with evil desire and hostile to God. *Scripture References: Ephesians 4:22–24; Colossians 3:9–10.*

Pornography: Any picture, video, story, or other media that we use to sin sexually in thought or deed against God.

Repentance: Turning from sin and turning to God in faith. Repentance is one aspect of the Triad of Life (faith, repentance, and love) that forms the basis of the Christian life. *Scripture References: Mark 1:14–15; 1 Thessalonians 1:9.*

Redemption: Specifically, it is the act of Christ purchasing and paying the price for his people through his death on the cross, and broadly it is the work of Christ for his people and in them. *Scripture References: Ephesians 1:7; Colossians 1:14; Hebrews 9:12.*

Same-sex attraction: Any romantic and/or erotic desire for someone of the same sex.

Sanctification: Sanctification is both 1) the once-for-all act of a believer being separated from his former way of life, spiritually dead and enslaved to sin, and being transferred into a holy status unto God, spiritually alive and freed from slavery to sin and 2) the ongoing process of being morally transformed in righteousness and holiness by the Spirit. *Scripture References: 1 Corinthians 6:11; Hebrews 10:14.*

Sex: Differentiated from biological sex, see above. Sex is any action or behavior with another that involves the stimulation of the sex organs.

Shame: A social status or feeling of dishonor and disgrace. Other words that can be included here are feelings of otherness and dirtiness. Shame is different than fear in that fear has to do with punishment and consequences, shame has to do with our social status and feeling between God and ourselves and ourselves and others.

Sin: Nonconformity to God's law. *Scripture Reference: Numbers 5:6–7.*

The Spirit: The third person of the Trinity, one in essence and distinct in person from the Father and the Son. The Spirit applies the benefits of our salvation to us. *Scripture References: Matthew 28:18–20; John 7:37–39; Romans 8:26–27; 1 Corinthians 2:10–11; 2 Corinthians 13:14.*

Suffering: Anything done to us as a result of the broken, fallen world in which we live.

Temptation: Any enticement to sin that can come from within us and from outside of us. *Scripture References: James 1:14–15; 1 Thessalonians 3:5.*

The Tree Metaphor: Harvest USA's model for understanding the human person, including our hearts, contexts, desires, worldviews, and behaviors, especially sexual sins. *Scripture References: Luke 6:43–45; Romans 1:22–25; James 1:14–15.*

The Triad of Life: The basis for the Christian life: a daily pursuit for faith, repentance, and love. *Scripture References: Matthew 22:37–40; Mark 1:14–15.*

Transgender: A broad term that does not view gender as binary in nature (people being either male or female) but sees gender as a spectrum. The identity label, transgender, is adopted by individuals who reject the traditional view that personal identity is associated with biological sex.

The Two Great Commandments: Love God and love others. The Two Great Commandments form one aspect (love) of The Triad of Life (faith, repentance, and love) that forms the basis of the Christian life. *Scripture Reference: Matthew 22:37–40.*

Worldview: Any foundational view of God, ourselves, and others that works itself out into actual behavior in life.

Harvest USA's mission is to bring the truth and mercy of Jesus Christ by:

- Helping individuals and families affected by sexual struggles
- Providing resources that address biblical sexuality to individuals and churches

We are a donor-supported ministry, so the churches and individuals who partner with us make it possible for us to produce resources like *Alive: Gospel Sexuality for Students* and provide direct ministry to individuals and families, free of charge.

If you found this book helpful, consider partnering with us financially, advocating for our ministry in your local church, and/or praying for our work.

For free resources, please visit harvestusa.org.

Harvest USA
715 Twining Road, Suite 200
Dresher, PA 19025
215-482-0111
info@harvestusa.org

Also Available from Harvest USA and New Growth Press

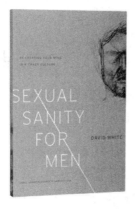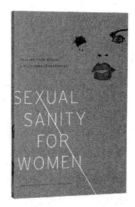

An eBook leader's guide is also available for each small group resource.

Coming in August 2018!

15-Session Video Curriculum
with Leader and Participant Guide

NEW GROWTH PRESS

Publishing Gospel-Driven Books to Build the Body of Christ

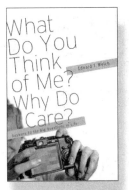  

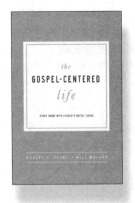  

newgrowthpress.com